What's being said about *How Many to Change a Light Bulb?*:

It's hard to judge a brilliant book, but I shall say: "stimulating, suggestive, and impressionistic." There is a saying: "Take it from someone who lived the experience, better than from someone who studied the experience."
—Elsayed Hussein, MD

David Parker tells his own story of overcoming debilitating depression and procrastination. Drawing on his own experiences, he offers powerful strategies for overcoming procrastination in simple, direct language, amply illustrated with stories and reinforced by techniques that you can easily practice on your own. It is written in an easy-to-use, step-by-step format and explains clearly and persuasively how and why his methods work. He developed The J.O.T. Method as a logical and task based response to his own depression and habitual procrastination. As a therapist with extensive experience working with students (amongst whom procrastination is extremely common) and depressed individuals, I would certainly recommend Mr. Parker's method to my clients.   —Alanna Cheyney, LCSW

I would recommend this book to anyone who tends to put things off and never seems to find time to achieve their goals. The book provides a simple yet effective way of organizing chores into doable activities. The tables in the book give the reader a clear illustration of how to put the techniques described into everyday practice. The J.O.T. Method provides positive feedback from day one and if used properly, will end your days of chronic procrastination.   —Martin Shack, LCSW

It's easily read as David talks to us, sharing his story without pretence. I am looking forward to sharing it with others.
—Helayne Neri-Cherin, BSN, RN, Complementary Medicine

(continued...)

Procrastination is an all too common, self-sabotaging behavior pattern, which affects every aspect of a procrastinator's life. David Parker's personal revelation of his own profound procrastination and ultimate renewal sheds valuable light on this subject, from a lay perspective so many procrastinators know all too well. He shares his many insights and personal hurdles on this subject, and provides a simple, yet effective behavioral technique in better management of this self-destructive behavior pattern. So don't procrastinate any longer—start reading!

—Ronald Yamamoto, Psychotherapist

To ERICA LIEBMAN,
SINCERE THANKS TO YOU FOR YOUR EDITORIAL
WORK AND SUPPORT IN HELPING BRING THIS BOOK
TO FRUITION! BEST!

How Many
Procrastinators
Does It Take
to Change a
Light Bulb?

Take Control
of Your Life
and Defeat
Immobilizing
Depression!

David Parker

DBP
Darwin Bay Publishing
Brooklyn, New York

Book design by Pete Masterson, Æonix Publishing Group, www. aeonix.com.
Main text set in Adobe Minion Pro, heads and tables set in Myriad.
Cover design and cartoons by Rick Menard, www.RickMenard.com
Author photo courtesy of Isidro Torres.

This book contains health information of a general nature obtained from scientific
and medical sources believed to be accurate. However, this book is not meant to
substitute for, and should not be used in place of, the health services available to
you from your own licensed physician, psychiatrist, psychologist or other health
care provider. This book should not be used to diagnose, care or treat any medical,
psychiatric, psychological or behavioral condition. If you believe you are suffering
from some sort of illness, you are strongly advised to consult your own physician
or other health care provider.

The J.O.T. Method™ is a trade mark that belongs to David Parker.

Publisher's Cataloguing-in-Publication Data

Parker, David, 1960 –
  How many procrastinators does it take to change a light bulb? Take control of
your life and defeat immobilizing depression / David Parker.
    p. cm.
    Includes index.
    ISBN 978-1-935880-00-4
1. Procrastination--Psychological aspects. 2. Depression, Mental. 3. Time management. 4. Self-realization. 5. Work --Psychological aspects. 6. Students --Time
management. I. Title.

BF637.P76 P37
155.2/32—dc22   2010931303

Published by:
Darwin Bay Publishing
Brooklyn, NY
www.DarwinBayPublishing.com

Printed in the United States of America

Acknowledgments

I WANT TO THANK MY editorial assistants Rachel Mann; Erica Liebman; and Anthony Battle; with a special note of thanks to George Gillson for early editorial advice and support. Extra special thanks to Miya Chu; John Colabro; Felicia Mattera; and Gina Tuzzo-Argenziano for their loving encouragement when this book was only a dream; and most especially to James Langton for setting a trail ahead for me to follow. Thanks also to Pete Masterson for design assistance; to Rick Menard for his cover illustrations; to Isidro Torres for the rear cover photograph; to J. Naomi Linzer Indexing Services; and Adrienne Bashista for providing CIP data.

I want to thank Lloyd Gelwan, Esq. for his many years of friendship; Sam Nole, CPA; Edgar David Grana for acting as my creative mentor; therapist extraordinaire Richard Clayton; Peter Victor, MS, MA, CH; and The Venerable Puntsok. Extra special thanks to my radio friends Geoff Fors and Jerry Abrams for keeping me company while this book was being written.

Thanks also to: Elsayed Hussein, MD; Kenneth Reddan, PhD, LCSW; Martin Shack, LCSW; Alanna Cheyney, LCSW; Ronald Yamamoto, Psychotherapist; Helayne Neri-Cherin, BSN, RN, Complementary Medicine; and Hamid Moussavian, MD.

A word of special thanks to Joe Baldizzone for sharing his thoughts on the creative process; to Lilly Kirschner for sharing her "Now—go accomplish!" philosophy; to Steven Kirschner his positive attitude, to Edward Harris for his warmth and support; and to Pamela Dixon for her feedback. Thanks also to Naomi Levinson for her goal-oriented approach to life; and to James and Crystal Kanellis for their support. My thanks to Rita Bell; Louis Friel; Joe Giunti; Kim Murphy; Bert Pittari; Martin Norregaard; and Elina Shnayderman. I also wish to thank the membership of the Greater New York Independent Publishers Association (GNYIPA) with extra-special thanks to Perry Brass and Heidi Russell; and the New York Center for Independent Publishing (NYCIP). Loving thanks to my sister, Lynne Dempsey.

Thanks to the following individuals for their help: Valentina Janek; Lana Smart, Evelin Gomez, and Nia Garcia at Just One Break, Inc. (JOB); Fredda Broza of the Federation of Employment Guidance Services (FEGS); Alice Pang, Angel Colon and the faculty and students of Stuyvesant High School, Manhattan; Warren McDowell and the faculty and students of The High School for Environmental Studies, Manhattan; and the faculty and students of Global Enterprise Academy High School, The Bronx. Thanks also to Jonathan Applefield; Joseph Castelli; Carlston Gray; Mary Lamanna; Herb Klein; Joseph D. Korman; Ellen M. Kozak, Esq.; Yujian "Eugene" Liu; Melissa McLaney; David Tanner; and Gail Wein.

A note of thanks also to my worldwide circle of Internet pals: Sally Benay; Paul M. Cicchetti; Emily Elkins; Jade de Guzman; Tim Gerard; Christine Lennis; Deborah Lockhart; Victoria Messler; Ian McInally; Mariana Muniz-Fraticelli; Toyia Phillips; Shauna Catherine Riley; Betty Samuels; Samantha Sanders; Michael Solomon; Juliana Tabak; Juanita Zealey; Allison; Axel; BizzSavvy; Donna; Jane; Ken; Liz; Mary; Sarah; and Yanti; and several anonymous friends.

Special thanks to The Portobello Road Help Centre (www.helpcounselling.com) in London; and The Maytree Centre (www.maytree.org.uk) also of London; and very special thanks to the Central London Branch of The Samaritans (www.samaritans.org).

Dedication

This book is dedicated to Dan Buckley.

At a time in my life when I was short on belief in myself,
Dan gave me what I needed most—
a strong dose of faith in my own abilities,
which gave me the courage to keep moving forward.

Thanks, Dan!

Contents

Introduction

WHILE WORKING AT MY DAY job as an administrative assistant in midtown Manhattan, co-workers passing my desk would sometimes give me a wink and a nod and ask, "So, how's that book on overcoming procrastination coming along? I'll bet you just can't find the time to get around to it!" You wouldn't believe some of the good-natured ribbing I endured.

However, if my co-workers had only known the extent that I had changed, I bet that instead of having winks in their eyes, they'd have had winces on their faces. Perhaps, because of my personal transformation from a dyed-in-the-wool habitual procrastinator, into the kind of person whom I like to refer to as a "do"-er. Having been such a habitual procrastinator, the completion of this book is a remarkable achievement because it wasn't so long ago that I had stopped taking care of many of my day-to-day responsibilities; something you'll read much more about in the coming chapters.

In fact, I had been a habitual procrastinator for so long that even today, years after having studied business administration in college, I can still recall when I first learned I needed to spend several semester-hours in their "Accounting Workshop." Funny as it may sound, I put off entering that room until the day I overheard a fellow student refer to it as "Accounting Lab"—somehow, that name change made all the difference for me. I suppose there was something that I truly disliked in that most-dreaded of all the four-letter words, "w-o-r-k."

So profound was my change, I soon wanted to discover if other procrastinators' ways of thinking and behaviors were similar to my own, and it didn't take me long to discover that many did. One early observation I made was how habitual procrastinators are generally impatient—due to their desire for instant results. Another observation was how their minds reconstruct the tasks they don't want to deal with, into negative scenarios—each accompanied by logical explanations and predictions for why those tasks couldn't possibly be accomplished. It's for these reasons that I have endeavored to keep this book as brief as possible by emphasizing clarity, brevity, and most importantly, **solutions**.

If you've read other self-help books, you may find this one to be a bit different than others. For one thing, this book doesn't concern itself with quick fixes. You won't find any magic wand solutions within its pages, and you also won't find a plethora of pop quizzes.

Some books that purport to deal with procrastination offer only half-hearted efforts. Instead of providing a comprehensive understanding of procrastination and how to overcome it, they:

> ➤ Treat habitual procrastination as though it were merely an annoying nuisance that can be defeated by employing cheerleader-like rallying cries such as, "I want you to put your foot down—for once—and for all! Ready! Go for it!" If only it were *that* easy.

> ➤ Encourage their readers to construct "to-do" lists without regard as to how they should deal with those tasks.

> ➤ Attempt to shame, beg, cajole, or belittle the reader into taking action.

Still other books would have you believe that the secret to overcoming procrastination is by learning to delegate one's tasks. That might do if your boss provided you with a personal assistant or if you hired a housekeeper, but it wouldn't teach you anything about overcoming procrastination because it only makes someone else responsible for your mess.

Your goal here is to overcome procrastination by learning how to deal with the things you've put off and, in doing so—to regain your self-esteem, which is a natural by-product of personal responsibility.

This book is divided into two sections:

> ➤ **Section One** explores why we procrastinate, how procrastination can develop into a habit, and how it can diminish your self-esteem by leading you into feelings of depression, anxiety, helplessness, and hopelessness.

> ➤ **Section Two** deals with the how-to's of overcoming procrastination. While many procrastinators are convinced that they can think their way into feeling better, non-procrastinators know that we can only act our way into feeling good—and that over-analysis leads to paralysis. Section Two looks at changing old behaviors by considering new methods of "do"-ing. You'll discover that completing small tasks is the way forward. That no matter how insignificant some tasks may seem, with each and every accomplishment you'll not only be handling the things that you weren't able to in the past, you'll also be restoring your self-esteem.

While you could start out by reading Section Two, I believe you would inadvertently miss out on important background material concerning procrastination, which is why I recommend that you start reading from Section One.

All that changing from a procrastinator, and into a "do"-er takes, is the willingness on your part to challenge your beliefs. As you gradually incorporate changes into your life, new feelings of self-esteem and personal pride will replace old feelings of depression and gloom which came about as a result of not taking care of your needs.

Even if you've grown concerned that you may have lost the ability to act on your own behalf, I can assure you that you can regain a great deal more control over your life than you might otherwise believe. This has been my own experience.

It is my sincere and heartfelt hope that this book helps you to start undertaking the tasks you've been putting off. In the end, not only will you become a "do"-er, you'll also discover that taking care of yourself generates positive feelings which you'll come to relish.

So then, "How many procrastinators does it take to change a light bulb?" The answer is: "None. Procrastinators sit in the dark!"

I wish you every success on your journey into the light!

Understanding Procrastination

Chapter One

A Life in Such Perfect Conflict

P EOPLE ARE PEOPLE. WHATEVER CULTURE we may hail from and no matter our differences, there are extra-special times when many of us share the same traditions. Two of these traditions arrive hand in hand every New Years' Eve, and nearly all of us can relate to them both.

The first begins just a few hours before midnight, as thousands of revelers gather in public squares to ring in the New Year. The second tradition follows close behind, as an army of news reporters brandish microphones and stroll the sidelines to ask celebrants the time-honored question: "Do you have any New Year's resolutions you'd like to share with our audience?"

Alcohol-fueled responses containing wish lists of hopes, dreams, and aspirations follow. Who among us hasn't heard:

> ➤ "I want to make more money!"

> ➤ "I'm going to lose 25 pounds!"

However, we almost never hear someone say:

> ➤ "I've been dissatisfied with the fruits of my labor, so I'm going back to school to learn some new skills."

> ➤ "Lately, I've been reducing sweets and snacks in favor of healthier things—but what I need is to find is a 24-hour gym in my neighborhood."

Given that today is the "age of the sound bite," those last two responses would likely be edited out of a news report, as though it's been accepted and determined that the public only wants quick and easy solutions to its problems and issues. One by-product of this artificially sweetened brainwashing is the public's general attitude of "What are you going to do?" resulting in an unspoken acceptance that the most important matters of the day are beyond anyone's control. This may seem to be a subtle form of procrastination, yet one needs only to glance at recent voter turnout reports to see a downward curve, ending in all-time low numbers. Simply put, a great many people don't show up to vote on Election Day because they don't believe that *their* votes *count*. That downward curve may end on a statistician's chart, but the trend itself reverberates through society.

One knock-on effect of this type of societal procrastination is similar to the new strains of super-bacteria that have grown stronger as they've grown resistant to antibiotics. It's today's career-politicians who have lost their fear of not doing the people's will, upsetting the electorate, and being kicked out of office. After all, if no one shows up to vote them out of office, what consequences do they face?

When citizens stop taking action as a group, what happens, and what effect does this have on how we feel? Politicians divert their attention to the wishes of their true supporters, political action committees that provide campaign contributions from big business interests. Is it any surprise then when politicians vote in favor of lowering business regulations, and we then read news reports of peanut butter infected with salmonella bacteria, and of contaminated gourmet pet food causing kidney disease and deaths of our cats and dogs? We stare in wonder, as the world seemingly spins out of control, and feel hopeless and helpless.

The same holds true with regard to how much or how little control we exert over our own lives. If we neglect our needs, we feel poorly as a result, and should we continue this neglect, we may begin questioning our resolve. For many, this is the start of a long, downward slide into mental depression.

A Procrastinator in Motion—Is Going Nowhere, Fast

Many procrastinators feel separated from the rest of society, one they may perceive of as having an almost instinctive knowledge of how to take care of its tasks and responsibilities. The procrastinator feels cold, remote, and detached from others, who he sees as capable "do"-ers. As a result of his procrastinating, he not only feels inadequate to others, but worse, he may worry that he's becoming incapable of living any other way of life. Most of the time, he feels *stuck*, especially when faced with a complicated task, or one that he perceives of as being *boring*.

For example, there were many times in my own past when I felt so overwhelmed, I simply froze and could not take action. During one particularly difficult and prolonged occurrence of procrastination, I telephoned a local crisis hotline due to the shame I felt when I realized that I was stuck mid-way through the job of plastering and painting the studio apartment I had moved into a few weeks before. Even worse, I began to worry that I might not be able to complete the job.

My furniture left me little room to negotiate, and I had never before taken on such a complicated job. One wall was half-puttied, while another that had been brushed with primer almost glowed in the dark, and the apartment reeked of plaster dust. Bed sheets covered my belongings and just lifting the sheets momentarily, resulted in small clouds of dust rising up into the air. It was a terribly depressing scene.

Hoping to prompt me into action, the hotline's volunteer asked, "How about this? Can you just picture how nice your apartment will look, and how good you'll feel after you've finished painting it?"

"No," was my simple reply. No other word had the same clarity and honesty to express the way I felt. The only thing I could picture in my mind's eye was myself as an utterly inadequate adult, and I was certain that this unfinished nightmare of a job could be done better and faster by just about any other person. So convinced was I of my inadequacies, the only outcomes I could foresee were either an apartment that looked worse after the paint job, or one that looked mediocre at best. In my twisted logic, it simply made no sense to continue, and for long periods of time I did nothing except to watch television while I internally cursed myself for my past bouts of inactivity; doing nothing to alleviate my situation other than distracting myself from this self-imposed misery.

During that time, it never seemed to occur to me that this was my very first experience in painting an apartment, especially one that first required extensive plastering, then a coating of primer, and last but not least, paint. Perhaps it might have been better to stop, assess the situation, and if necessary, hire professional painters and observe how they did the work, preferably from an easy chair. But I was stuck in the land of procrastination, and even if it was in spite of myself, I was determined to finish the job.

Somewhere between *somehow* and *eventually*, I finished painting my apartment. I recall feeling good for a short while, and feeling a sense of relief as well. However, as soon as that warm glow of satisfaction began fading, in its place I began reviewing, examining and criticizing the efforts that had brought that job to a close:

> ➤ "Why didn't I finish it sooner?"

> ➤ "It really wasn't that difficult, was it? Why am I so dumb?"

> ➤ "What's wrong with me?"

The typical habitual procrastinator lives in a self-contained and depressive world that, for the most part, consists of unrealistic expectations, broken self-promises, and frustration. We target ourselves with character assassination by placing unrealistic and unattainable demands upon ourselves. Plodding through life, we harbor anger at what we perceive of as an uncooperative world filled with people who seem more able and more capable of routinely coping with tasks—the same tasks that drive us to distraction. Yet, for the most part, our anger is directed at ourselves.

Procrastinating in the Workplace

Although I don't know for certain the exact moment in time when I first began procrastinating, I can easily recall many times when it caused me great upheaval. Once, while working as a temporary office assistant at a television network in midtown Manhattan, I failed to see what all the fuss and bother was about a contract that needed to be sent overnight to Hollywood.

The next morning my supervisor came by, and she appeared more appalled over my lack of concern about the contract, still lying on my desk, than for the contract itself. Although I can now see that her concern was justified, I recall thinking at the time, "If it was so important, why did they trust it to a temp in the first place?" By the time of that incident, procrastination had already ingrained itself into my life so thoroughly that it hadn't occurred to me that my job wasn't just about taking care of *things*, like contracts, which I hadn't done: it was more about taking care of *my employer's needs*. It almost goes without saying that my job lived up to its name—"temporary," and ended just a few days later.

Another time, a lawyer, whom I was assisting, complained that I spent too much time trying to figure out how to "do" something, rather than just "doing it." Once again, I was only able to see the situation from my perspective, which left me wondering how one is supposed to simply "do." At other moments, supervisors griped that although I did my work, it took me too long to get things done. While I strove to keep my emotions in check, I focused on the basics of my job, cringing whenever a superior suggested that I undertake a new responsibility. Here are some other comments I received in the workplace:

> ➤ When faced with a task, I made "mountains out of molehills."
>
> ➤ One supervisor told me she suspected that I was "avoiding work."
>
> ➤ Another supervisor complained that I "thought too much."

Indeed, many fellow procrastinators have told me that they've stared in amazement at co-workers who not only juggle the demands of a full-time job, but also take care of several children at home before and after work. It's people like that for whom the adage, "If you want something done, give it to the busy person," not just applies, but makes so much sense.

Procrastinating at Home

Not all procrastinators are the same. Some complain that while they have no problem with procrastination in the workplace, they find themselves immobilized by some of the simplest home-based tasks. They often say things like, "I *do* whatever is asked of me at work by my superiors. Anything they ask, and I do it. So you'd think I would *do* for myself at home, now wouldn't you? I mean, if they told me to stand on my head for ten minutes, I'd do it, if I could—so long as they paid me for my time. Still, my home is a mess and sometimes I worry that a co-worker might invite me over for a party at his or her place, especially around the holidays—and that I'd feel obligated to return the favor. What would I do then?"

Another sufferer said, "I have a large stack of newspapers sitting in a corner of my kitchen. Every morning I do the same thing: I go in there to make coffee and then, I see *it*. I tell myself, 'This weekend, I'm going to tackle that.' But then, when the weekend comes, I say to myself, 'I'll be dammed if I'm going to deal with *that mess* on my day off. I've got better things to do. I can't be bothered with that right now.' Of course, Monday morning rolls around again and then I walk into the kitchen to make coffee. The moment I see that pile still sitting there, well—I could cry. Then, I think to myself, 'Not again! Why didn't I take care of that mess over the weekend? What on earth's wrong with me?'"

Another common home-based scenario happens when a procrastinator worries there isn't *enough time* to finish everything he wants to accomplish. This in turn can lead to frustration, which can result in the avoidance of all productive activity and essentially, in shutting down. This *all-or-nothing* reaction is a *coping mechanism* that can quickly become habitual in nature, occurring whenever the procrastinator finds himself with spare time that otherwise could be put to use. One reason behind this automatic reaction is that many procrastinators have a poor sense of time, most especially, with *personal* or *free time*. What the procrastinator is really dealing with is the feeling of panic that results from having *some time,* because he has never learned how to effectively manage his free time. Not knowing how to cope in a situation that he's been in many times before, he does the only thing he know, he panics, and then attempts to flee from these terrible feelings—substituting action for anything else, which is the act of procrastination.

Habitual procrastinators earn the title of *habitual* by practicing their craft steadily over a lengthy period of time, and as a result of this practice, they often have many undone tasks that require attending to. When the procrastinator has a bit of free time, he thinks of all that he's put off and quickly becomes overwhelmed. "How could anyone jam years' and years' worth of tasks into a spare twenty minutes of free time?" he wonders. If you are a procrastinator, you may be asking, "So then, how do you get several years' worth of tasks done in such a small amount of time?" Stay tuned. In the second half of this book, you'll learn how to develop positive ways to cope with, and accomplish, your tasks.

Science Experiments in the Kitchen

Some readers might find this next procrastination example to be a bit hideous while others will hardly bat an eyelash and say, "Yeah. Been there—done that." During one of my lowest points I stopped dealing with one of life's necessities, the dishes. My kitchen sink was completely filled up with dirty dishes, used knives, forks, spoons, cereal bowls, coffee cups, pots, pans, and plastic food containers. Shortly thereafter the drain became clogged and stagnant water began accumulating in the sink.

It was the weekend, and I got by on fast food while putting off the task of dealing with the dirty dishes. Soon the unpleasant aroma of rotting food and foul water began to make its presence felt whenever I neared the sink, especially after mold had begun growing inside some of the containers. When I came home from work that Monday evening, I faced something that had the look and smell of a *science experiment* growing in my kitchen sink.

Annoyed at the mess, I reacted by doing the only thing a skilled and practiced procrastinator could do. I put my coat back on and went out into the brisk and chilly November evening to a twenty-four-hour convenience store to purchase a supply of paper plates, plastic utensils, and Styrofoam cups.

Looking back on it now, it's difficult to decide what was the oddest aspect of that situation. Was it my refusal to deal with the dishes at the start, or how I had allowed the sink to get into that condition? Or, perhaps worst of all, why did going out to buy those disposable items seem like the perfectly logical action to take? After all, which would have taken the greatest amount of energy: cleaning the dishes, or going out into the cold night air to go shopping for plastic ware and paper plates after coming home from a long day at work?

What's funny about this situation is that by avoiding the problem in that way, I delayed having dinner far longer than if I had just stayed home, cleaned one pot, began cooking, and then cleaned the rest. However, at that particular moment, my actions actually did make sense to me because not only did I not want to deal with the dishes—I also felt "I just couldn't."

In reality, I could have washed the dishes, however, by habitually procrastinating, I had convinced myself that I really *was* incapable of cleaning the dishes at that particular time, and probably as much in the foreseeable future too. In other words, as long as I had my disposable utensils, I no longer had an *immediate need* to deal with the situation in my sink.

"After all," I rationalized, "I paid good money for those items—so, I might as well make use of them." And, there the clogged sink stood, its contents secure, while the mold continued to grow. A few days later a more distinct odor began wafting from the sink and it was only when the stench became overpowering that I finally gave in, cleaning the accumulated items, not with dishwashing liquid but with scouring powder—all the while wearing long rubber gloves.

Even Though "I Did It"—"It" Doesn't Really Count

Much to my own dismay, there were times, albeit rare ones, when no matter how difficult the task—I not only *did* it, but surprised myself at my ability to deal with unappealing tasks that I had put off for great lengths of time. This often happened with regard to housecleaning.

The rule concerning these all-out clean-ups was that they were permitted when, and only when, they were due to *external forces*. Their cause was usually for one of the following reasons:

➢ Friends were coming over to visit.
➢ Relatives were coming over to visit.
➢ A girlfriend was coming over to visit, especially when it was a new girlfriend.
➢ The landlord was coming over to visit.
➢ The building's super, plumber, a cable television installer, or some other type of handy person was coming over to do work in my apartment.

As far as I was concerned, doing a concerted "clean-up" under these circumstances just didn't count, even if my place looked nicer for the effort. After all, the only reason I accomplished the task in the first place was because I worried, "If they see how I live, they'll think, 'He must be a *nut*,'" or, "If the plumber tells my landlord what condition my apartment is in, he might try to have my lease revoked."

Of course, once the special event passed, it was back to business as usual, with me playing the hapless, helpless, and, essentially, hopeless procrastinator. However, even if it was just for a short while, my apartment looked like it belonged to the person that I yearned deep inside to be. In the span of time between when I began to clean up and when the last guests left, I saw that I really hadn't lost my ability to make my place presentable. Instead, it seemed more that I had simply abdicated myself from that responsibility.

At the start of this section, I mentioned that, "Much to my own dismay, there were times, albeit rare ones, when no matter how difficult the task—I not only *did* it, but surprised myself at my ability to deal with unappealing tasks that I had put off for great lengths of time." To be honest, perhaps I wasn't quite as surprised as I was *bothered*. Bothered, because of the undeniable proof that I was actually capable of "do"-ing many of the tasks I had already convinced myself that I was utterly incapable of undertaking, let alone successfully completing. So, despite how much I might have told myself that a smaller task "didn't count," nevertheless, its successful completion counted a lot more than I gave it credit for.

Isn't Procrastination a Fancy Name for Laziness?

As a procrastinator, there were a few occasions when practically all sense of my personal responsibility to myself seemed to fly out the window. I may have showered, shaved, and wore clean clothes, but that *me* was the one I presented to the world—the other *me* was a disaster. Not only was my apartment a mess, but my bills went unpaid until I received a second or third notice. Delaying the bills left me feeling overwhelmed, and during periods when my bills were left unpaid, nervous confusion and stomach pains plagued me. While I knew that I *should be* paying bills, I couldn't bear dealing with them because just about every part of the process seemed to require too much effort. At the same time, the more I put off—the more I had to do.

Seeking understanding, comfort, and a bit of insight into my condition, I talked to trusted friends, neighbors, and with professionals in the mental health field. To my chagrin, every once in a while someone would ask, "David, are you sure that you're not just being lazy?" All right, fair question—but my answer is a resounding "No." Why? Let's take a look at the following chart:

Procrastination	Laziness
➢ Procrastination is a long-term condition. It can last for years and stay with a person into the future without end.	➢ Laziness comes and goes. The lazy person has far more control over his condition than the procrastinator could ever dream of having.
➢ The procrastinator feels regret over his inaction and says, "I should have," "Why don't I?" and, "Why didn't I take care of that when I had the chance?"	➢ The lazy person acknowledges his situation with, "Yeah, I'm lazy, that's me!" safe in the knowledge that he will act, long before it's absolutely necessary.
➢ Procrastination involves the cessation of important and even essential activities. A procrastinator may discover that he has run out of food or come home to no electricity because he hasn't paid his bill for months.	➢ While a lazy person may put things off, he also keeps one eye on his deadlines. He may come close to disaster, but he gets a jolly thrill after coming close to the edge of the falls, while not going over the side.
➢ The procrastinator is very unhappy with his way of life and wants to change, but he doesn't know any other way of life.	➢ The lazy person is quite satisfied with his life and is generally as happy as anyone else. He's apt to sum up his situation with, "It's no big deal!"

As we can see in the above chart, there are several differences between procrastination and laziness. The first difference is that procrastination is a long-term problem. Many procrastinators complain that they've suffered with the condition for years and don't have any expectations of living any differently. On the other hand, many persons who accept that they have a lazy-streak often claim that it's not a big an issue for them because their laziness comes and goes over time, depending upon how involved they care to be. A second point is that the procrastinator is puzzled by his errant behavior: "I know I should take care of my needs, and I know what those needs are—so, why don't I take care of them?" Conversely, the lazy person is the first to admit to his situation, because he knows full well that when he needs to act, whether he wants to or not, that he will.

In addition, many procrastinators find difficulty in keeping track of important future dates, like appointments, even when they may be charged for those missed appointments. Lazy people usually have their needs firmly planted in their mind's eye and rarely, if ever, completely let things go. Lastly, generally speaking, procrastinators can be a glum lot because they constantly carry the burden of all the things they should have taken care of, and they don't trust themselves to "do" any better in the future. In contrast, lazy people have more of a laid-back "I'll get to it," lifestyle. People who are just lazy aren't terribly concerned with their chosen lifestyle because they know that in time they will eventually get to whatever *it* is, just as they've done many times before.

A Growing Problem

Before my problems with procrastination became habitual in nature, there were times when I delayed taking action and whatever opportunity may have been lost, the most significant and costly loss was the effect upon my self-esteem. Even if the task were relatively simple, such as mailing back a pre-paid postcard within a time limit, I would misplace the card, forget about it, and then find the postcard after the offer it promoted had expired. Afterwards, I would think, "No one else on earth could have goofed-up like *I* just did!" There were many such times when brilliant opportunities were lost—forever. One might think that after enough such occasions, I might have learned my lesson. Unfortunately for me, quite the opposite happened: my problem grew.

You may have some personal experiences involving the squandering of precious opportunities, and you may be wondering if your own procrastination has been more than just a passing fancy, and more like a bad habit. The short answer to this question is: If you believe that you have a problem with procrastination, then you probably do. However, should you want more of a quantitative measurement, then look for the combination of:

➤ How frequently procrastination occurs.
➤ How many areas that procrastination crops up in your life.
➤ How strong your opposition to "do"-ing is.

It's this across-the-board aspect that really determines how much impact procrastination can have, and the extent to which it plays a part in a person's life.

We all have obligations of various types. Bills need to be paid, bank statements need to be reconciled against checkbooks, and even making time to watch television programs can be a balancing act. No matter how simple our tasks may initially appear, many, if not all of our tasks require thoughtful action; and it's for that reason many people find procrastination to be a never-ending burden.

I usually had a variety of tasks that I simultaneously procrastinated on. Typically, it wasn't that I procrastinated about *certain things*; rather, it was more that I procrastinated over just about *everything*. For example:

> ➢ I put off visits to doctors and/or medical tests for months—all the while worrying about the condition of my health.

> ➢ Before leaving home for work I would do a mad scramble searching high and low for my wallet, house keys, cell phone, and pen. I sometimes wondered if there was some special medical classification for persons like myself, who were unable to leave home because they couldn't find their house keys? Was this actually agoraphobia, the fear of leaving home, in disguise? No, I thought. I was trying to leave home, not to remain in it.

> ➢ Bank statements sat in their unopened envelopes on the kitchen table until I had accumulated several months of them. Supposedly, this prevented me from losing valuable free time to a mundane chore like balancing my checkbook. Unfortunately, while putting it off, I had to rely on the bank balances that I obtained from ATM receipts. Usually, it was the fear that the bank might have made an accounting error that would finally prompt me into action and it was then that I faced with the enormous job of having to deal with reconciling six months or more of bank statements and ATM receipts.

> ➢ Utility bills awaited payment because of the drudgery involved in having to sit down, write checks, and deal with my unbalanced checkbook.

> ➢ Clothing of all types was draped around my apartment in various and often-inventive places, while several days' worth of socks lay scattered across the floor.

> ➢ Like many habitual procrastinators, being a perpetual latecomer was virtually a *lifestyle* for me.

> ➤ I recorded countless television programs but never made time to watch them. Making matters worse, instead of writing down what I had videotaped, I merely kept a vague notion in my head of what had been recorded. As one videocassette filled up, yet another one was started. One by one, the tapes would build-up and in my twisted logic and rationalization, I would begin deluding myself that the videocassettes contained only second-rate programs because they could not have been *worth* watching if I hadn't done so when the programs first aired. It never seemed to occur to me that to have a chance to watch those programs, what I really needed was to begin structuring my time—even if it was my leisure time.

In short, by avoiding my tasks, I expended more mental effort and energy than those tasks would have taken had I only dealt with them in the first place. Unfortunately for me, like many procrastinators, I was still on the decline and still had a long way to go. I was now putting off so many different types of tasks that my problem with procrastination not only grew unchecked, but I also began feeling overwhelmed by my emotions. As a result, my inability to deal with my tasks led to another inability shared by many sufferers of habitual procrastination: that of feeling unable to cope with the enormous despair that I felt over my situation.

Being Carried Along by the Tides of Circumstance

A habitual procrastinator's life is akin to the voyage of a rudderless boat, afloat and underway, yet with the ability to steer and command a course. In much the same way, the procrastinator aimlessly negotiates the waters of life, forever allowing the tides of circumstance to have their way with him.

As an adult procrastinator, I often felt like a child lost in a sea of adults. Similar to when I was a five-year-old in Macy's department store and strayed too far from my mother and felt bewildered by the seemingly mountainous range of countertops and endless shopping aisles: *"Mommy! Mommy!"* I cried out in fear of abandonment. Adult procrastinators act in a somewhat similar fashion, but instead of *crying out*, we cry *inwards* by internalizing our feelings of inadequacy and bewilderment through a continuous stream of negative self-talk and self-admonishment.

Like many procrastinators, I carried my negative feelings with me, day in and day out, almost as if I were carrying the proverbial "weight of the world" on my shoulders. Here's just a partial list of the sort of judgments I made against myself:

> I felt as if "I didn't have all my marbles."

> I not only lacked confidence and respect in myself, but was also convinced that other people "must have" seen the same in me.

> Overly burdened by the matters I had put aside, as well as my inability to deal with them, I sometimes felt as if I were living in a dream world, unattached to reality or other people.

> Procrastination wore me down and felt akin to a bad cold. I often felt tired and sluggish, as though every task took all the energy in the world to complete.

> Many times, when just the thought of dealing with an anxiety-provoking task came to mind, I would automatically associate that thought to a negative scenario. For example, just before sitting down to scour the on-line classified ads and job-hunt, my mind would conjure up the scenario of sitting in the dentist's chair, or of dealing with an awful drudgery, like housecleaning.

> I had no sense of the word *priority:* only crises, deadlines, and external demands prompted me into taking action.

> Many, if not most of those crises, were of my own making in the first place. By waiting around for disaster to strike, there'd come a time when I simply *had to* act, and this gave me the perfect excuse to break through the shame that kept me immobilized. However, so far as I was concerned, I was only dealing with them because once again, the evil forces commonly known as "them" had forced my hand.

> Focusing on only one task at a time was enormous task in and of itself. Whenever I tried to force myself to deal with one task, other tasks I had put off would come flooding back into my mind, as if everything was a priority and needed immediate attention.

> I felt afraid most of the time. Overwhelmed, I avoided feeling fear and anxiety through various means, like television, food, alcohol and recreational drugs. However, by furthering my avoidance, I not only made my original problems worse, but created other problems as well.

> It was as though I was waiting for "David" to do come and do it. Still, who exactly was "David," and where was he? And why wasn't "David" taking care of "me"?

> There almost seemed to be two of me…"Irresponsible Me" and the more rare, "Responsible Me." A poet might have called it: "A life in such perfect conflict."

Spinning hand in hand forming a psychological vortex were two of my worst attributes: an inability to select a single priority to work on, and difficulty focusing on just one task.

Memorial to an Unknown Adult

My difficulties in being able to focus on just one task led to all sorts of problems. One example of this was the piles of papers that grew in various places in my apartment. The largest of them sat on my kitchen table, while smaller piles on shelves resembled birds' nests.

These piles were made of all sorts of things, but many of them consisted of items plucked from my wallet: store receipts, cash machine receipts, fast-food coupons, and names with telephone numbers jotted down on scraps of paper. Besides that, the piles also contained a good deal of unopened mail, like bills and bank statements, plus restaurant menus that had been slipped under my door and hastily scribbled notes that I hadn't yet dealt with. It was those handwritten notes that were my greatest cause of frustration. How could I have so many of them, what should be done with them, and where should they go?

Where did they come from? What do I do with them all? Which do I keep and which should I toss in the trash? What if I threw out something I should have kept? All these questions, plus my lack of answers, caused terrible feelings, such as bewilderment, confusion, fear, frustration, and anger, within me. That last emotion, anger, was the one that bothered me most, because I wasn't terribly certain if my anger was directed at those bothersome stacks of papers, or at myself.

Each time I glanced at them, they almost seemed to eerily communicate back, mocking me. Sometimes, I'd make a half-hearted attempt to take action upon them by combining the smaller piles into one large paper mountain of sorts. Of course, just one look at this staggering heap was too much, and I'd quickly walk away from it and do something sensible, like turning the television on. For me, this mountain awaiting action became something of a "Memorial to an Unknown Adult."

One evening, full of self-loathing, I confessed this inability to function normally to a neighbor. He drew a breath and said, "You're bigger than those stacks of papers, David. Just do it!" My neighbor's words made me feel worse.

The two of us batted the topic back-and-forth like a tennis ball. He would say, "You have power over these things." Then I'd reply, "But I don't have power over them; that's my problem." Of course, the very next day my paper mountain grew a bit larger. As it grew, I lost even more faith in my abilities, and in myself. To be certain, I was up the creek—without a paddle or a guide.

Fed up with the papers, as much as with myself, I would occasionally take an action, of sorts. I would briskly sift through the mountain, combing through it and plucking out anything that had no purpose whatsoever. These were usually things like fast-food restaurant coupons that had already expired, and store receipts from the most insignificant of purchases. Then I would begin segregating what was left over, sometimes by subject matter, other times by size. Finally, I'd re-stack the items neatly until they resembled more of a neat and well-proportioned pyramid than a craggy and old paper mountain. My work done, I would once again retire to my television set.

What does this tell us? For one thing, it tells us that when a procrastinator has ample time to deal with a task that he's put off for a while, he will often choose lower-priority *wants* over higher-priority *needs*. For example: in the scenario above, the priority I chose was to half-heartedly deal with that paper mountain as quickly as possible, a *want;* rather than doing what I truly *needed* to "do," which would have been to actually deal with it until I had essentially eliminated it.

Unfortunately, nothing that actually required effort was dealt with, and of course, the next day I would again at the stack and think, "Why didn't I take care of *that* when I had the time? What's wrong with me?" This self-doubt and shame at my perceived inadequacies led to an even greater lack of confidence in my decision-making ability, which then led to even lower self-esteem, and to even more task avoidance. With all of this against me, should I have been surprised to find myself falling into depression every now and then?

Habitual Procrastinators Can't Afford the Luxury of Free Time

I can recall an occasion when a two-week vacation from work was approaching, and I eagerly looked forward to using the entire time to clean and organize my apartment. Anticipating abundant time and energy to mount an all-out assault on untidiness, I began formulating my strategy:

> ➤ **Day One:** Remove everything from the smaller closet, throw out what I don't want or need any longer, mop it down to remove the dust, stick a fan in there to air it out, go out for pizza, then return to put what's left back in, and enjoy the extra space!

> ➤ **Day Two:** Tear apart the larger closet, do the same as day one, get pizza from a different place and make mental notes on who made better pizza while basking in the glow of another clean closet!

> ➤ **Day Three, etc.:** More elaborate plans involving cleaning and pizza!

Need I tell you what I accomplished during that vacation? I'll give you one guess… are you ready? Absolutely nothing!

So what did I do with my precious time off? Well, an awful lot of it was consumed by watching television, and by counting the days I had left in my vacation. Not surprisingly, I returned to work feeling tired and emotionally bogged down by this defeat at my own hands.

Today, not only do I find myself amazed by what I put myself through, but I've also been surprised and humbled by many individuals who have related similar tales. Habitual procrastinators often have difficulty in managing our free time, and when we do a poor job of it, we tend to suffer emotionally. Conversely, we often flourish when we're placed under rigid conditions, like final deadlines, which helps explain why some of us do well in the workplace while we do poorly at home.

Complex Conundrums

If you began a weight-lifting program and continued your new regimen over time, would you be surprised if you noticed increased muscle mass and strength? Of course you wouldn't. This is merely a common example of the positive relationship that exists between exercise and fitness. In much the same way that exercise strengthens muscles, every time we delay taking action, we are simultaneously developing a *mental muscle* of sorts, we could think of it as our "procrastination muscle."

Imagine for a moment, a person visiting his doctor and complaining about feeling listless, or lacking the energy to deal with his chores. He then goes on to mention that procrastination has become an annoying part of the lackluster period that he finds himself in. Generally speaking, the medical community often sees procrastination as one of a number of symptoms that relate to the condition of mental depression, and rightly so because procrastination is a symptom of depression.

However, if a person procrastinated for a very long time, what levels of happiness and self-satisfaction would you expect to see in that person? Do you think you would see such a person as having high self-esteem or low self-esteem? Although I am not a health professional, as someone who has suffered first-hand with procrastination as a long-term debilitating condition, I believe procrastination is not merely a symptom of depression, but it can also be a direct cause of depression in some individuals. For a person like myself, whose last name is not followed by "M.D.," the most scientific name that I can come up with for the kind of immobilizing procrastination that I and other procrastinators have suffered from, is a "conundrum." Simply put, it is my belief that there is an inverse relationship between the conditions of procrastination and mental depression. In other words, as the habit of procrastination becomes pronounced and grows stronger, the sufferer's self-esteem can weaken to the point where he feels hopeless, helpless, and terribly depressed.

If this wasn't bad enough, there is yet another conundrum where procrastination can be observed, and that is through its similarities to the condition known as Obsessive-Compulsive Disorder (OCD). It has only been in the last few decades that OCD was at last recognized as a disabling condition in its own right. Today, it is generally defined as a psychiatric disorder characterized by obsessive thoughts and compulsive actions. For our purposes of defining OCD, we can think of *obsessions* as recurrent and persistent thoughts, while *compulsions* are repetitive behaviors and mental acts.

Interestingly, procrastination has aspects of both branches of OCD; in other words, one can find both obsessions and compulsions within the procrastinator. For example, a procrastinator might obsess over a past inaction by thinking, "I should have taken care of those bills yesterday; why didn't I do it when I had the chance?" At the same time, his behaviors can also mimic the compulsive component of OCD because before taking action, he backs off, saying to himself, "I know I should sit down and pay the bills right now, but I don't feel like it. I'll do it tomorrow!" So, procrastination can not only take the form of either an obsessive thought or a compulsive behavior, it can also be a complex mix of both components, working together as a disharmonious tag-team helping to propel procrastination to its highest heights.

The Good News—Change Is Possible

So then, the question needs to be asked: If habitual procrastination has been such an all-encompassing, formidable, and difficult foe, how could a person such as myself wind up writing a book on overcoming it? Luckily, although I may have stopped taking care of myself at times, I was not incapable of observing and eventually changing many of my negative behaviors, which resulted in my ability to produce this book.

Truth be told, there are still times when I am approaching an unfamiliar task that I may feel some degree of apprehension. However, the difference between then-and-now is like the difference between night-and-day, because today I don't allow feelings of fear or anxiety to get the better of me. During my transformation from procrastinator into "do"-er, I began to find a new sense of balance, and as the process continued, I noticed myself feeling a bit more comfortable in my own skin.

If you work at overcoming your own habitual procrastination you'll start overcoming the fear that has interfered with your ability to deal with the tasks and projects that you've learned to automatically shy away from. You'll discover that you are far more capable than you thought possible, and your new definitions of yourself will be based upon newer self-beliefs garnered from positive experiences.

Actively procrastinating is like stumbling through life like an ill-prepared actor. When I was a practicing procrastinator I sometimes wondered, if I were miraculously transformed into what I would have called a *regular person*, how I would look back on my earlier life? Would I hate myself for all the opportunities I'd lost, and if so, what would I do with all the anger that I imagined would come? Having bridged that gap, I now find myself at peace with those times. All I can say is that I simply did not know any other way of living.

All You Really Need Is Willingness

Giving up a long held belief or lifestyle, even one that works against you, isn't easy. Beating up on yourself doesn't help, nor does trying to hurry the process along. Like a cigarette smoker who only *wants* to stop smoking—but never gives stopping an honest try, wishing alone doesn't help, because wishing is not a strategy. What does help is learning to do things differently, and then giving those new ways a real chance by trying them out. In short, it's all in the "do"-ing.

Change is possible. As you will see later, the key ingredient that you'll need to provide is willingness. Change takes place slowly and over a long time. It's essential that you give yourself patience in order to continue growing into the person you want to become. You'll also need to treat yourself to love and understanding. As a friend pointed out to me, "Ask yourself this question. What would do if you loved yourself?"

If you are a habitual procrastinator, the "spell" that you've seemingly been living under can be cast aside and believe it or not, the power is in your own hands. As the second half of this book reveals, becoming a "do"-er is a lot more than merely possible. You'll learn practical ways that will teach you how to deal with many of the tasks you find unpleasant or beyond your present ability to cope with. All it will require on your part is the willingness to practice some new ways of "do"-ing.

Chapter Two

"How Did I End Up This Way?"

THIS BOOK HAS ITS ORIGINS in a special type of diary called a "feelings journal" that I started writing on a cold and gray winter morning while living in London. Although I'm a native New Yorker or, to be accurate, a humble Brooklynite, I was unemployed on that gloomy London day, and renting a sparse room in a low-budget hotel—separated from my then-wife, as well as my friends back home.

I was suffering through a prolonged and devastating mental depression, and my spirits seemed as low as the clouds that clung to London's low rooftops. Feeling under pressure because I was low on money, every morning I awoke to panic attacks—talk about your morning jolt! Typically, there were three types of days I muddled through:

> ➢ Those on which I was very depressed.

> ➢ Those when I suffered though anxiety and panic attacks, but didn't feel terribly depressed.

> ➢ And the days when I suffered through panic attacks while feeling greatly depressed for most, if not all, of the day.

Although I had had quite a long history of depression back home, my living circumstances in London contributed greatly to my heightened level of distress. An old adage goes, "Be careful what you wish for, you might get it!" That resonated within me because although it had once been my dream to live in London, my dream had turned into a living nightmare. Not only was I attempting to cope in the midst of a terrible depression, I was running out of money as well. If that wasn't enough, I also had to deal with my new cultural status, that of being a foreigner. Despite the fact that I had visited London many times prior to relocating there, another old adage rang true: "It's one thing to visit a place, and another thing to live there."

Just months earlier, I had been hospitalized there for depression. However, "depression" was too mild a term for what I had been going through. What actually landed me in the hospital was a strong desire for permanent relief from all the difficulties that I had faced for far too long.

Living in that foreign locale, I was alienated to a large degree and even worse, I had far too much free time on my hands. Hoping to reduce my woes by talking them through, I visited the walk-in center of The Samaritans, where I would chat about my troubles with a kind volunteer. I also availed The Caravan, a free counseling center on the grounds of St. James Church, just a short stroll down the road from Piccadilly Circus. These gracious strangers helped me to continue moving forward through that sad, desperate period of dark despair.

"Feelings, Nothing More Than Feelings"—Or So the Song Went

Stuck in despair, I tried to recall anything that might help my situation. I remembered that when, years earlier, I was in a similar depression and a friend had recommended that I keep a feelings journal as a way of tracking my moods from day to day. I began that journal because, in spite of the help that I received at the counseling centers, I continued to feel emotionally shattered and unable to pull myself together.

Ironically, there were some occasions when I felt slightly worse after a counseling session than I'd felt before the session had begun. Of course, this was never the intended effect of a session, and in spite of this infrequent and unintentional backlash, I was grateful for the concern those volunteers showed me, as I still am today.

It seemed that since conventional talk therapy focuses on how the client, or *myself*, in this case, generally feels while in the session, that after spending thirty minutes focused on exactly why I felt so poorly, I sometimes left a counseling center feeling somewhat more unsettled than before I had entered it.

It felt as though I had fallen into a deep, dark hole—and it eventually occurred to me that perhaps I alone, might be the only one who could help me find my way out of it. So I began writing that feelings journal as a kind of self-constructed ladder, to help me climb a path of self-discovery and betterment.

The Procrastination Cycle

Eventually, I found a job in London, but although my financial pressures let up a bit, I was still very depressed. Despite living in one of the world's most cosmopolitan cities, my daily routine consisted of going to work and then returning to my hotel room, only to spend the entire evening watching television. It seemed that I was completely content to living a life of dull misery. Although a good part of me desired a change for the better, I felt utterly hopeless.

I continued writing in my journal and as time passed, I accumulated enough material to begin taking a look back at what I had written, and this presented me with an opportunity to observe the ways and patterns in which my mind worked. For the most part, each page consisted of sad thoughts and fears of tomorrow; however, mixed-in and almost hidden from view were hastily scribbled *reminders,* or "to-do notes." Most had been quickly jotted down and just as soon forgotten. There was no logic or telling as to where they might appear—they just popped up and then disappeared with the turn of the page. Perhaps rather than "to-do notes" they were actually "here's stuff you still haven't gotten around to doing notes."

A few days later, I was reviewing my journal again when, suddenly, it seemed like something unusual had occurred, it was as if all those *reminders* had connected in some odd way, but only momentarily. The connection appeared to me for only an instant, and then…whoosh…it was gone. This happened every time I re-read the journal, however, the more I saw it—the clearer it became. There seemed to be a relationship between the length of time a task was left undone, and the effect it was having on my emotions. This connection was so real; it felt almost palpable—as if I could run a finger over each *reminder* and *feel* the extent to which it affected me. Imagine that each *reminder* were a wire carrying its own electrical current—while one offered the faintest perceptible buzz, the next one might feel like high voltage. In reality, these pseudo-shocks that I *felt* were actually parts of me getting in touch with my feelings about myself. These feelings ranged from,

"When am I going to get around to that?" blues, to "I wish I hadn't written that down!" panic.

One of these *reminders* in particular clearly stood apart from the others: it was an unpaid bill from a warehouse back in the U.S. that was storing my belongings. Paradoxically, seeing this *reminder* unleashed on me a torrent of self-anger for not having dealt with the task, while at the very same time, I still didn't want to deal with it! I was frozen in place and felt paralyzed, like a rabbit caught in headlights.

If that wasn't enough, I couldn't find a better reason for not paying the bill other than, "I didn't feel like it." After all, it wasn't like I didn't have the money to pay the bill—I was working. It had more to do with the fact that I hadn't balanced my U.S. checkbook in several months, and I didn't know what my bank balance was. So, my burden from procrastination was greater than I'd originally thought, because there was just *no way* that I was going to deal with balancing *that checkbook*.

You might think I had a relatively simple choice to make here by either dealing with it then and there, or deciding to continue suffering in misery. However, I found neither of these two options viable, because I simply didn't want to deal with it at all. So, I did the only thing that I knew would work for me: I distracted myself by turning on the television in my hotel room and channel-surfed until bedtime. Meanwhile, the storage bill waited for the next time I happened to stumble upon that *reminder*.

Unfortunately, while I could divert my attention from my tasks with relative ease, whenever I attempted to deal with just one task, one of the following scenarios usually played out:

> ➢ If I tried to focus on just one task, then the other tasks I had put off came flooding back into my mind, causing me to second-guess myself about which one I should *really* be doing.

> ➢ If one particular task felt "impossible" to complete, I then felt incapable of accomplishing any of them.

> ➢ Once in a great while, but usually on a Saturday or a Sunday, I'd wake up and decide that *that day* was "the day" to tackle my tasks—meaning, all of them. It didn't take very long for me to realize I didn't have the patience to deal with just one of them, let alone all of them.

Soon, my ever-decreasing ability to handle tasks, combined with ever-increasing levels of frustration, led to lower levels of self-esteem and stamina within myself, which culminated in feelings of mental depression. In short, not only did I worry about my ability to complete tasks—I also grew concerned about my ability to take care of my own well being. Self-pity then turned into self-anger and I berated myself with terrible self-judgments, such as "I'm a worthless piece of crap," or, "I'm unworthy to roam the earth among other people, the ones who have value and take care of themselves." My self-directed anger then boiled over and I reluctantly came to the belief that, as a person, I was *incapable.*

Upon reaching that conclusion, an unexpected feeling of serenity came over me. It seemed as if there was no longer any point in beating myself up, for it was all quite obvious: that compared to other adults, not only was I *incapable,* but *inadequate* as well. Thus, doomed to this terrible fate, it seemed rather cruel to continue beating up on "poor old me." In light of the circumstances, it made a lot more sense to be kinder to myself, and to even treat myself to some much-needed *relief* as a compensation of sorts for all the pain, anguish, and misery that I'd just gone through. Can you guess what form that took?

Would you be surprised if I told you that it was spending countless hours watching television? Actually, there were many times when my self-inflicted wounds needed healing from similar traumatic experiences and I would either bathe my psychic injury in alcohol ("Poor me, poor me, pour me another one."), smoke marijuana ("But only on days that ended in the letter *"y"*—like *Monday,* and like *Tuesday,* and like *Everyday.*"), or I would engage in overeating ("I feel better when I feel filled!")

Getting back to that storage bill: after a couple of days' escape from reality, I always had a clever solution at hand with which to buy me a little more time. For example, I could do the courteous thing, by calling the warehouse's accounting department from London and saying something along the lines of, "I'm sorry but I think I'm a little behind in my storage bill—it must be a terrible burden for you. I'm really a bit ashamed to be telling you this." The bookkeeping clerk would actually be grateful for my call, and then compliment me on my "honesty." This usually bought me enough time to formulize a plan to accomplish the unthinkable, if not the unbearable: calling my bank in New York to find out my checking account, writing a check, and then mailing it to the warehouse.

Of course, after this drama had run its course, I'd eventually discover, or rediscover, yet another source of discomfort, whether it was a tax form that required completion or one of those *reminders* that I had stumbled upon while reviewing my journal. Whatever the particular task was didn't matter too much, because I had long since convinced myself that as a person, I was both inadequate and incapable.

Looking back upon all of this, I can now see that what I had believed were a series of individual incidents, were actually the same situations that were happening with different scenarios and people. My distress, which was rooted in procrastination, would come and go over time, and came and went in the form of "Procrastination Cycles."

Here's how each "Procrastination Cycle" ran its course:

1. I had numerous tasks which required my attention, but which I avoided.
2. If I were reminded of a task, I became enveloped by anxiety, especially by the tasks I had put off longest.
3. My level of anxiety rose steadily as I worried: (a) that I was unable to complete the task; (b) that I was also uncomfortable with the task; (c) that I didn't have the patience to deal with the task; (d) that I might not "do it" correctly.
4. Feeling psychologically paralyzed, physically weak, and utterly helpless about situations that I felt I had no control over, I fell into a state of depression.
5. After anywhere from a few of days to a few weeks of this internal confusion and conflict, I reached the point where my self-pity turned into self-anger, and I berated myself for not attempting what I believed *I should be able to do.*
6. Eventually, it seemed almost cruel to continue torturing myself for what seemed like an inborn weakness, and I came to peace with the fact that I was incapable of taking action. I then reasoned that I needed to go easier on myself and instead, to give myself some much-needed tender loving care, like watching television, surfing the Internet, or indulging in comfort foods or mind-altering intoxicants.
7. Returning to reality, I eventually rediscovered the task that I had fled from. If I happened to be under a time constraint, then I devised an action plan of sorts.

8. Otherwise, I continued to disregard the task and "The Procrastination Cycle" was once again underway.

After you've gone through The Procrastination Cycle a few dozen times, you gradually become a different person because despite evidence to the contrary from when you have accomplished tasks, you've already convinced yourself that you're utterly incapable of handling much of anything that requires patience, thought, or action. Over an extended period of time, habitual procrastination leads to ever-declining energy levels, which in turn can lead to feelings of depression. If you have any doubt about the relationship between procrastination, energy levels, and depression, ask yourself if you've ever heard of a habitual procrastinator who's been described as a "highly-energetic individual."

When I was a habitual procrastinator, although I wanted more out of life, I suffered from ever-declining reserves of energy. Not only did I feel incapable of handling the simplest of tasks, I also felt incapable of living any other way of life. I began to see myself as *locked* into a lifestyle that I did not want, much like a drug addict who sadly realizes that his habit has turned the tables on him. Not only did I now feel helpless, but hopeless as well; feeling even less like the adult I should have been. Like many people in this situation, although I was acutely aware of my depression, I didn't see the role that procrastination was contributing to my low moods.

In London, upon continued reviews of my journal, I kept noticing how those *reminders* affected my moods and emotions. The longer that those *reminders* had been put off, the greater the effect that they had upon my feelings. It became clear to me that I was on to something: there was a definite relationship between my problem with procrastination and the depression that I suffered from. Oddly enough, while procrastination is usually seen as a *symptom* **of depression**, I observed that **procrastination was *causing* my depression**. As I began thinking about this relationship, I realized that I needed to look a bit more closely at procrastination itself.

Procrastination—A Most Unusual Word

"Procrastination" is a somewhat deceiving word because it starts with the prefix "pro," which we naturally associate with concepts we favor. For example, Jerry says: "When it comes to auto safety legislation, you can always count on me to be on the "pro" side. Whether it's seat belts, air bags, or some new technology, if it makes driving a safer experience then I'm all for it!" We can also find "pro" within words that represent positive benefits, like "promotion," "protection," and "provide." So then, why would such an annoying and debilitating condition like procrastination begin with such a positive-sounding prefix? Wouldn't a better way to describe *delayed doing* be "anticrastination"? Well, on second thought, perhaps not!

In actuality, the troublesome area of the word "procrastination" is found in its second half, that "crastination" part. It comes from the Latin "crastinus," which means, "to put off." When the parts are combined, "procrastination" takes the meaning of "In favor of putting off." For the average person, this straightforward answer makes perfect sense. However, for habitual procrastinators, it's a partial definition, because their concepts of tasks, time, personal responsibility, and how they interact are quite different from most persons'.

How is a Habitual Procrastinator Different from Other Persons?

For most of us, procrastination can be defined as: not getting things done, even when we know that we *should* do them, whether or not we've considered the consequences of continuing to put those tasks off.

In fact, for many, procrastination is a casual and passive practice. If you live in the United States, you're probably aware that April 15th is called "Tax Day," because it's the day by which income tax returns must be postmarked. In New York City, last-minute tax-filers race up the stairs of the General Post Office while an actor dressed as a giant aspirin bottle prances comically in front of the building. Television crews interview the late filers, who give statements like, "I made it!" or, "I'm never going to put myself through this nonsense again, never!" This is an example of casual procrastination, which everybody does at one point or another. It's no big deal.

While anyone can casually procrastinate, there are other persons who procrastinate to a much higher degree. These people are habitual procrastinators. Habitual procrastinators put off many different tasks that encompass a wide variety of tasks, chores, obligations, and responsibilities. A habitual procrastinator may say that he has "a thousand and one things that he needs to attend to"; however, he not only continues to let them go, he's also constantly aware that these unattended-to duties are causing him great anguish. In comparison to casual procrastination, we could call this active procrastination, which might seem like a contradiction of terms—after all, can anyone "actively not-'do'"? Habitual procrastination becomes *active* when it becomes extremely pervasive in a person's life. For example, there are some habitual procrastinators who can easily come up with a list of twenty important tasks they're currently aware of, which they need to get to. There are also other habitual procrastinators who could say, "You've got only twenty things you need to get around to doing? That's nothing!" Let's look at two gentlemen, Stan and Charlie, and see how they handle similar events.

Stan is a casual procrastinator, as much as just about anyone else is. One day, he notices that he must be developing a cavity because he feels a sensation of acute pain in his upper jaw. He doesn't particularly like the thought of going to the dentist, so he puts up with the pain for a few days while summoning up the courage to make an appointment. When the pain worsens two days later, Stan calls the dentist's office, schedules a prompt appointment, and has the cavity taken care of. Upon leaving the dentist's office, Stan says to himself, "What a relief."

Then there's Charlie, who is a habitual procrastinator. Like Stan, Charlie feels the same sort of toothache and, also like Stan, he dislikes the thought of visiting the dentist. However, unlike Stan, Charlie puts a good amount of effort into not seeing his dentist by going to a drugstore to buy a pain reliever. Although this buys Charlie a few weeks away from the dentist's chair, eventually the pain becomes so bad that he's forced to make an emergency dental appointment. At the dentist's office, he discovers that he now has an abscess that requires extra work. The dentist comments, "You must have been in pain for a while—why didn't you come in sooner?" When Charlie leaves the dentist's office, he says to himself, "Why did I put that off for so long? I'm such an idiot!"

If we look further into this comparison, we can see that while Stan temporarily allows himself to delay his visit to the dentist in order to buy a little time, his own tolerance for this delay is actually quite low. We can almost imagine Stan saying to himself, "It's time to get this taken care of before it gets worse, because you can't fix it yourself."

Now let's take a closer look at how Charlie handled the same situation. Over-the-counter pain relievers play a role in almost everyone's life at some point, but when Charlie went to the drugstore it wasn't so much to obtain a bottle of tablets, as it was to avoid the need of visiting his dentist. He then continued using the pain reliever for as long as he possibly could to keep from seeing the dentist. While Stan believed that he couldn't imagine dealing with a cavity on his own, Charlie's decision was quite the opposite. Then, after unbearable pain indicated that Charlie's coping-mechanism had failed, he was then faced with the news that he had an even worse problem, an abscess, which required extra work. Then, for seemingly the millionth time in his life, he heard, "Why didn't you have this taken care of sooner?" Here we see another aspect of habitual procrastination: a refusal to learn from past mistakes. In fact, if there's just one thing Charlie's heard more often, it's "Well, I just hope that you've learned a lesson from all of this." Charlie just hates it whenever somebody says that to him.

One more difference between the casual and the habitual procrastinator can be found in the areas of self-hate and anger. Remember, after leaving the dentist's office, Stan thinks, "What a relief," while Charlie berates himself with, "Why did I put that off for so long? I'm such an idiot!"

Indeed, while Stan is relatively proud of himself for handling an uncomfortable situation as best as he could, Charlie leaves the dentist's office not only angry at himself, but angry at the dentist as well for his comment. Of course, the dentist didn't mean to embarrass him, but, like many of us, Charlie doesn't like facing the consequences of his inactions. Another reason behind Charlie's anger is that with so many uncompleted tasks in his life, Charlie didn't have time to visit the dentist. Not that Charlie ever gets around to those tasks, he doesn't; however, that never stops him from using his burden of undone tasks as an excuse for not having the time to get around to dealing with any of them.

While casual procrastinators usually visit the same dentists on a relatively regular basis, many habitual procrastinators may believe it's been so long since they've seen one that they feel as if they no longer have a regular dentist. Other procrastinators grow concerned after a long absence from any dentist's office that their teeth will either look so bad, or require so much work, that they might face the same sort of comment that Charlie received. To counter this, some habitual procrastinators resort to making emergency appointments with dentists they've never been to before. In a habitual procrastinator's way of thinking, if the dentist were to make such a detrimental comment, it won't matter as much because chances are, he'll never see that dentist again.

One last difference between casual and habitual procrastinators is that casual procrastinators are often more apt to express remorse when they've inconvenienced someone than a habitual procrastinator would. This is because habitual procrastinators actively abdicate their adulthood, and so display little regard for orderliness, timeliness, consequences, or for the feelings of others. When they're forced to deal with matters, they're often angry with whomever or whatever is requiring them to respond responsibly. Although they are very angry with themselves, they often internalize that anger—if they feel embarrassed, pressured, or put upon, they may occasionally hurl an insult to save face. Let's take a look at some additional aspects of habitual procrastinators.

The Act of "Getting Over"

Simply put, habitual procrastination is not taking care of one's needs on an ongoing basis, except when forced to by external circumstances; however, this malady also has a political meaning. By "political," we are not referring to government, taxes, or to voting on Election Day, but to the relationships that we have with others.

Many habitual procrastinators have remarked that they began noticing what they could get away with from an early age. This practice is commonly called *getting over on others,* and many procrastinators have mentioned to me that they engaged in this behavior, and that it may indeed relate to their current procrastination. For example, when I was a boy, I wanted to *get over* on my mother because I did not like being ordered by her to brush my teeth. I rebelled against that responsibility by pretending to brush my teeth—recreating the sound by swirling my toothbrush inside a plastic cup filled with water, emptying out the cup, and repeating this several times while the water faucet was going full-blast. In reality, much like our friend Charlie's attempt to avoid the dentist, I put more energy into the act of *not doing,* than if I had simply brushed my teeth in the first place.

As time passes, if we continue the act of *getting over* on others, it can become difficult to put an end to this sort of practice. After all, who wants to give up a skill that they've worked hard at developing over a lifetime? Earlier in this chapter, I described how I gave that warehouse clever excuses for my delay in paying their storage bill. Now if that wasn't an act of "getting over" as it relates to procrastination, what is?

Habitual procrastinators are often latecomers too, and this is yet another way that we engage in getting over. Besides not taking the responsibility to show up on time, we often deny responsibility for our lateness by blaming things like late trains or heavy traffic. While concentrating on coming up with excuses, the habitual procrastinator doesn't take into account the other person's feelings because he's keen on getting across to that person that it's he, the procrastinator, who's been inconvenienced.

The Art of "Getting By"

Some procrastinators silently wish that their needs could be taken care of for them. For these people, procrastination represents a reluctance to stand on their own two feet as independent adults. Their procrastination may lead them to leave the competitive world, choosing instead the to try just "getting by" with as few hassles as possible. Procrastinating in this way might best be called, "resistance to progression in life."

As a result of this lifestyle choice, over time I slowly unlearned personal responsibility by living a life of minimal responsibility, which included getting to the very real point of irresponsibility on a few occasions.

Reasons For or Behind Our Procrastination

Having lived the life of a habitual procrastinator for quite a spell, I have long pondered the question, "How did I end up this way?" While communicating with other procrastinators via e-mail, I asked for their thoughts on this question. Here are just a few of their reasons for engaging in this debilitating habit:

➤ Wanting to avoid the dull sort of life that "responsible persons" have.
➤ By refusing to deal with a task, they feel more "in control" than when dealing with real situations, real people, and real consequences.
➤ Having a desire to rebel against bosses, parents, teachers, government agencies, or other authority figures.

> ➢ A lack of discipline growing up.

> ➢ Initiating action without prior preparation or plans, which often leads to frustration from unexpected problems, and to poor outcomes.

> ➢ Not having back-up plans, which can lead them to the belief that they are doomed to a life consisting only of "no-win situations."

> ➢ A difficulty in managing frustration. When this is the case, procrastination often feels like pressure-relief.

> ➢ Not having been taught coping or problem solving skills from an early age.

> ➢ Not having an internal rewards system in place to promote staying on-track. Without rewards, we have less incentive to forge ahead.

Stress and Procrastination

Sometimes life can be complicated and demanding. Many people who do not habitually procrastinate have a personal mental reserve of positive experiences that has been built-up from times when their coping abilities were challenged, yet they persevered until completion of the task. These personal reserves serve to make them stronger and better prepared for future tasks.

Many habitual procrastinators don't have the same sort of personal reserve because they usually have had fewer positive experiences that they can draw back upon. Often, just thinking about a task can create a feeling of almost paralyzing anxiety. This explains why so many procrastinators have a difficult time just trying to sit down to think over how they might deal with a task—for them, facing it is usually more than half the battle.

To counter this anxiety, the procrastinator may try rushing into action. However, he does so without a plan—and when we act without planning, we usually get off to a bad start and have even less chance of a successful outcome. In addition, feeling stymied from the start can often become a habit unto itself.

In the workplace, procrastinators often find tasks more emotionally draining than their non-procrastinating colleagues. For example, there were times when I came home emotionally exhausted from a difficult day at work and crept under the bedcovers to take a nap, only to wind up sleeping the entire night away. Although some might say, "You probably needed the rest." to me, it was not a restful slumber because I had lost that evening's free time, only to awaken and find myself facing another workday.

There were also many weekends that I lost by sleeping away a Saturday or Sunday afternoon on the living room couch, despite household chores that required my attention. Before nodding off, I would tell myself that I was taking a time-out break, and there were even times when, not caring if I slept the day away, I would lightheartedly call it "taking a snooze cruise." It was a bit like taking a little escape away from the world and one's responsibilities, except, as a procrastinator, in my case it was deliberately engaging in oversleeping as a method of handling stress. It's not necessarily one of the best ways to handle stress, because it's really just another form of procrastination.

Using Procrastination as a Coping Mechanism

The act of procrastination can be likened to how a cigarette smoker takes a smoke break because he "needs a *time out*." Just as cigarette smoking is a false option against stress, so is procrastination. In fact, the comparisons between the two are striking.

After all, why do people smoke cigarettes? Well, first of all, it's a habit, just as procrastination is. Second, it provides people with the illusion of reducing stress, while at the same time, creating a dependency on cigarettes, which, as almost any cigarette smoker will say, causes stress. Similarly, the procrastinator seeks relief from his burden of stress by delaying work on his tasks. Later, with his task still hanging over his head, he not only feels regret over his decision to delay, but, more importantly, he perceives himself as a weak and ineffective person. Does the procrastinator then change course and tackle the awaiting project? Of course not! Without a track record of successful endeavors, he once again avoids confronting his feelings. So, the procrastinator develops a dependency on procrastination. Just as a smoker may require a cigarette after undergoing stress, when a procrastinator feels stress he tends to *shut down*; however, this itself is procrastination, which leads to even greater levels of stress.

Over time, a person who possesses poor coping skills may adopt procrastination as his default method of stress reduction. Procrastination can become habitual when a person's initial response to a task is to shy away from it because he feels overcome or flooded by anxiety. This automatic response may provide temporary relief from anxiety; however, the more he avoids uncomfortable situations, the more uncomfortable he then becomes with anxiety. As a result, not "do"-ing becomes an automatic response to anything that causes distress. Instead of will power, "won't power" becomes the rule.

Sometimes a procrastinator will engage in a pursuit that has no real value just for the sake of having a substitute activity (such as aimless channel surfing or oversleeping) in order to calm down from the anxiety he feels. He can also distract himself from a task simply by thinking of other things, like by daydreaming. Here are some typical reactions to internal anxiety that habitual procrastinators often tell themselves:

➢ "I'd rather do it when I *really feel* like doing it; that way I'll be motivated, and do a better job."
➢ "I know I should be doing other things, but right now, I need to take a nap."
➢ "I can't deal with balancing that checkbook. I wonder if I'm missing anything on TV?"
➢ "I'm not doing the laundry now—I'll do it later."

Although we all need to take an occasional break at one point or another, if your breaks are just taken to avoid your responsibilities, then your procrastination can progress into a bad habit. Luckily, like most bad habits, it can be overcome if you make a solid decision to change. While that change cannot happen overnight, if your decision is firm, you can purposefully implement that change into your life—and you **will** notice the difference over time.

As you may have already noticed, procrastination is a highly complex system that develops and grows. It then becomes second nature and an enormous source of frustration within the person suffering from it. This sense of frustration often comes from self-directed questions like, "Why don't I do what I need to do, when I need to do it?" or, "What on earth is wrong with me?" Questions like these can seem so relatively simple and natural to ask that we may assume their answers will also come to us with that same relative simplicity. Unfortunately, nothing could be further from the truth.

We can ask ourselves about why we procrastinate until we're blue in the face, yet accomplish next to nothing. This is because habitual procrastination involves the thinking patterns and self-beliefs that we've developed over a long time. That's part of the reason why I decided to write this book, after numerous years of therapy yielded precious little in the way of positive results.

Procrastination as Self-Protection Against Threats

Some people become habitual procrastinators as a means of developing a protective mechanism against emotional overload. One root of their procrastination grows out of the concern that their tasks will be mentally trying or physically exhausting. They fear their tasks will drain whatever precious reserves of emotional energy they may have left, the ones that their overactive minds haven't already depleted from worrying. Procrastination then becomes habitual, and can escalate to the point where practically all tasks seem too difficult.

Here are some typical causes of emotional overload that we may procrastinate over:

> ➤ You put up with poor health, and delay visiting the doctor over concerns of being diagnosed with a serious illness.

> ➤ You put off balancing your checkbook out of worry that it might not contain as much money as you would like it to have, or because you become easily flustered at the thought of the totals not balancing up.

> ➤ After receiving your annual statement of earnings from the Social Security Administration you find errors in it, but postpone writing to them because you dislike dealing with large governmental agencies.

> ➤ You apartment is a mess. The windows need cleaning, the carpet hasn't been vacuumed in months, and the bookshelves need dusting but you're concerned that you won't have enough energy to do it.

> ➤ You've put off doing the laundry for so long that you've run out of clean clothes to wear. Still, you can't bear the thought of lugging several bags of dirty laundry over to the cleaners and spending hours watching the washing machines and dryers rotate.

> ➤ Your supervisor appears with two boxes of files and says, "It's your turn to deal with these." You really dislike filing, and your boss has personally handed these files over to you. Still, you wonder if there's a way you can flee from this unpleasant task without alerting him.

When procrastinators feel overwhelmed, they tend to go into self-protection mode, shutting down like overloaded circuit breakers do. However, while circuit breakers re-set at only the push of a switch, people are a bit more complex.

So, Why Do I Continue Procrastinating?

"I know I'm driving myself nuts by procrastinating about this, that, and everything. So, why do I *continue* doing it?" I've been asked this question by many procrastinators, and it's a natural question. Just why do we keep on procrastinating when it causes us so much stress? Well, for some pretty good reasons. Here's just a few of them:

➢ We've been this way for quite a while, and although procrastination is not the best coping method ever invented, it has helped us to avoid some stressful situations for better or worse—unfortunately, it's usually for the worse.
➢ Procrastinating makes us feel independent because no one can pin us down and force us to do things we don't want to.
➢ Our approach is to *hesitate-and-evaluate,* instead of *facing-and-embracing* those tasks that we perceive of being difficult or unpleasant.
➢ We're uncomfortable at the thought of facing disappointment.
➢ We feel more "in control" when not doing something that could otherwise challenge us, embarrass us, or cause us to feel frightened.
➢ We abhor those tasks that we perceive as being "boring" or "complicated."
➢ We are used to *burying our heads in the sand* as a response to stress.

It's worth mentioning that some people procrastinate for the buzz that their nervous system receives from stress caused by their own delays. For example, while leading a discussion on the topic of habitual procrastination at the Stress Relief Club of Stuyvesant High School in New York City, I posed this question, "Why do we continue procrastinating when we already know it's not good for us?" One student responded with, "I like the drama." He then added that by putting off his studying, he believed that he was giving his nerves "extra tension" in order to perform better on tests.

I asked if he thought this line of thinking was entirely true. "Entirely? No," he replied. He went on to say he worried that his belief in procrastination's merits might be his own rationalization. I suggested that although he might hope that he might feel that this buzz was sharpening his senses, he knew perfectly well what he should be doing, which was studying. Procrastination can seem to offer pressure-relief, but this is only an illusion because whatever buzz anyone gets from it, comes at the expense of stress, anxiety, and worry later on.

A habitual procrastinator can be somewhat of a miserable creature. Weighed down by a long string of unaccomplished tasks built up over the years, along with an inability to deal with his present tasks, he sometimes worries about how, or if, he will ever deal with the as of yet unknown tasks that will present themselves to him in the future. In addition, he may also worry about how his loved ones, friends, or colleagues perceive him. Is it any wonder if he occasionally feels depressed?

Avoiding one's tasks is akin to sweeping dirt under a rug, and you can almost picture such a sad soul, stubbornly kicking himself forward through life. In fact, one procrastinator said he felt as if he were wearing a large "kick me" sign on his back.

Let's imagine for a moment that you were a visitor from another planet who came down to Earth with orders to observe the behavior of Earthlings who habitually refuse to deal with their tasks. Needing data, you interview a few of them and notice that many of them not only complain about their own behavior, they also bear resentment for those times when they were forced to act due to circumstances beyond their control. This, despite the fact that they would have had control, if only they had taken charge earlier.

Wrapping up your study for presentation to the scientific community back home, you look for a name to describe this group of Earthlings. What name would you bestow upon this species?

Chapter Three

A New Species Is Discovered— The Human Ostrich

OVER TIME, AS I CONTINUED my self-exploration by jotting down my moods in my feelings journal, I began noticing a relationship between my difficulties in accomplishing tasks and my low feelings. Even when I had ample time to take care of seemingly smaller tasks, such as doing the laundry or going out for groceries, when I felt severely depressed there was often only time for hiding under the bedcovers and sleeping the day away. Suffering with low energy levels, the only other activity that both distracted me and ate up loads of time was endless television viewing. I felt utterly helpless, while hopelessly confounded by my own psychological condition, victimized by a foe that had control over nearly every aspect of my life—or so I believed.

Depression Isn't My Fault—Is It?

At that time, I believed that, whatever the cause, my depressive states were entirely beyond my control. However, in order for that to be true, those causes really had to be *beyond* my control—in other words, they had to be the sort of maladies usually deemed larger-than-life, such as:

> ➤ **Bad genes:** I had inherited a family history of depression, said the professionals. "You were born with a predisposition to depression," they said. As my fellow Brooklynite—Curly Howard of "The Three Stooges"—had insisted in a courtroom, "I'm a victim of soicumstance."

> ➤ **A rough upbringing:** I was a small, skinny kid in public school. Always the runt of the classroom, I suffered the taunts of schoolyard bullies and their troubled peers.

> ➤ **Disruption of my career plans:** From an early age, I had wanted to become a radio broadcasting engineer. I even went to a vocational high school in order to learn electronics, and then studied broadcasting at community college. It wasn't until I was attending college that I learned that the traditional position of broadcast engineer was being phased out due to automation. What teenager wouldn't become depressed after discovering that his dreams had been squashed?

> ➤ **Alcohol and recreational drug use:** In time, I discovered that if I didn't feel good about myself, I could at least *feel better* by getting thoroughly plastered or stoned. The only downfall to this was that while attempting to discover my inner-self, I allowed everything else to fall by the wayside.

> ➤ **Bad luck:** Well, if the combination of bad genes, a rough upbringing, disruption of my career plans, and alcohol and recreational drug use weren't bad luck, I ask you, what is? Obviously, I was doomed to a life consisting of struggle and strife.

There's an old tale about a snowy night, when an outreach team committed to helping homeless people found a man shivering in a bus shelter. After repeated attempts, they coaxed him into their van and took him to a local hospital for evaluation. Later in their shift, one of the outreach workers stopped by the man's hospital room to check up on him. It wasn't very hard to find him because he was repeatedly yelling at the top of his lungs, "Nurse! Let me out of here!" The outreach worker peeked in through the doorway and saw the man strapped to his bed, begging to be set free.

Seeing this, the outreach worker thought to himself, "How odd. A few hours ago this man was fighting frigid temperatures and now, he's laying on a bed with clean sheets and a blanket, demanding to be let back out into the cold." Then it came to him: "This man must have a great liability. No, what he actually has is a great *lie-ability*—an enormous ability to *lie to himself*." This personality trait can also apply to habitual procrastinators.

I Really Could, but Please Don't Tell Anyone—Most Especially, "Me."

One day, I began reviewing the pages of my feelings journal again because I wanted to find out why depression immobilized me to the extent that it did. I noticed that some of my writings detailed day-to-day activities, while others concerned tasks that I wanted or needed to accomplish.

On page after page, I observed that while some tasks always got done, the same was true in reverse as well. By this, I mean that no matter how much time I might have had, some tasks were never accomplished. My entries seemed to stare back at me from their pages, making me feel as if I'd inadvertently played cruel pranks upon myself; however, there they were, and in my very own handwriting! Among the notes jotted down about how poorly I felt was something else that, while unwritten, was irrefutable—the longer I had shunned my undone tasks, the worse my depression had grown.

Let's take a look at some of those tasks in a side-by-side comparison:

Although I Seemed Able To	I Seemed Unable To
➤ Shave, shower, and get dressed.	➤ Get to work on time.
➤ Search on-line personals ads for hours on end.	➤ Search on-line job ads for better job opportunities.
➤ File papers away at work.	➤ Deal with the small paper notes and ATM cash receipts that filled my wallet.
➤ Pay vendors at work by writing checks and making bookkeeping entries.	➤ Open bills and write checks at home.

The fact that some of the tasks I avoided bore an eerie resemblance to many of the things that I did for pleasure or self-satisfaction compounded my frustration. For example: in the above table, one entry refers to my apparent inability to search on-line classified job advertisements. Like many people, I disliked job hunting—after all, was anything worse than the humdrum tediousness of searching for a job? Along with the mind-numbing activity of scrolling through lists of jobs, you then have to reply to the suitable ones, trying to persuade potential employers that *you* are the best possible candidate. And, if reading their ad once wasn't "enough," I often needed to re-read it a few times to insure that my response addressed their needs, trying to be sincere without sounding needy, while trying to impress them with my experience while not wanting to come off as arrogant.

Perhaps the only thing that was worse job hunting was the very real possibility of facing rejection. The way I saw it, I faced two sorts of rejection. First, there was *silent rejection*, when I simply didn't get a response. The other sort of rejection occurred after I'd gone through all the trouble to dress up, show up for the interview, and wind up not getting the job. Who needed frustrations like those?

One of the ways I avoided the chore of job-hunting was by going on the Internet and getting lost for a while on dating web sites, searching the postings for a possible love interest. This I could do for hours on end. Let's examine how I conducted that particular activity:

➢ After going on-line, I would find a suitable personals web site.
➢ I would then begin my search either by scrolling through the postings one-by-one and saving the ones I liked, or by using a search filter to limit my selections to women who lived nearby or were age-compatible.
➢ Either way, that left plenty of ads to go through—and go through them I did!
➢ Upon closer examination, I usually found something that disqualified an ad from further consideration. In that case, it was simply on to the next one.
➢ One by one and posting after posting—I would go through a large assortment of ads from women who were seeking companionship.
➢ Every now and then, there would be one posting that made me stop and re-read it.
➢ I might even take the time to read her posting a third time, in order to make sure I understood what she was looking for in a companion.
➢ With her "talking points" in mind, I would begin crafting my response: trying to be sincere without sounding schmaltzy, while wishing to impress her while not presenting a falsehood.
➢ "There!" I'd think to myself with a flare of attitude, and even possibly a bit of confidence: "If she doesn't go for *that*, then I don't want her!"
➢ I'd then hit the "Reply" button for what I hoped might be a chance at romance.

> ➤ Finally, after considering the possibility that she might not take the bait, I'd go back to that web site and go through more personal ads.

Do you notice any similarities between how I went about job-hunting and how I went about looking for a love interest? Here are some of the co-incidences that I found:

While I Had Great Difficulty	I Seemed More Than Able To
➤ Spending time scrolling through Internet job ads.	➤ Scroll through Internet personals ads for hours at a time.
➤ Putting effort into responding to job ads with intelligence, honesty, and confidence.	➤ Put effort in responding to personals ads with intelligence, honesty, and confidence.
➤ Facing rejection because my résumé might be dismissed at first glance.	➤ Face rejection because my response might be dismissed at first glance.
➤ Facing rejection by an employer after the job interview.	➤ Face being rejected by a woman after the first date.
➤ Enduring the process of finding a job.	➤ Enjoy the process of finding a romantic interest.

What do we make of this? While I abhorred just the idea of getting down to dealing with some tasks, other tasks provided me with a sense of adventure, making me want to take a chance and be proactive, even when the outcome was uncertain. Moreover, while just the thought of job hunting made me feel overwhelmed and not in control of the situation, something else like searching through personals ads made me feel warm and motivated, despite the fact that these activities shared so many eerily similar elements.

So, I avoided some situations like job-hunting, where I felt uncomfortable because I felt like I wasn't in control, which in turn made me feel as if I were taking an unacceptable gamble with my free time. However, at the same time, I tended to gravitate toward somewhat similar situations, like going through on-line personals ads, where I also wasn't in control and had pretty much the same chance of a positive or negative outcome as job-hunting. In short, I had just as much control over my job hunting activities as I did when

I searched personal ads; it was merely my perception of the two activities that caused me to avoid one while becoming completely lost in the other.

Reacting—By Not Acting

When it came to tasks that contained a strong component of emotional fear, I had learned that it was a whole lot easier to put certain things off than to deal with them. The only thing was, I had become so used to feeling that way that there was no longer anything unusual about that reaction. It seemed as if I was automatically reacting—by not acting. It wasn't that the task was getting the better of me; it was more the apprehension that I would become fearful which kept me frozen in my tracks. After pondering this for a while, I recalled the words that President Franklin D. Roosevelt said at his inaugural address on March 4, 1933: "The only thing we have to fear is fear itself." That summed things up perfectly.

It then occurred to me that I was behaving like the stereotype of an ostrich. As the cliché goes, an ostrich buries his head in the sand upon the slightest inkling of fear. This age-old notion about ostrich behavior, though, has actually been long since disproved. What people believed was an automatic reaction to fear was actually a different activity altogether. As part of their eating routine, ostriches dig small holes in the ground and forage for pebbles, which they swallow to aid in the digestion of their food. Of course, if ostriches really buried their heads in the sand after sensing danger, their entire species would have died out long ago due to an inappropriate response to predators.

Nevertheless, the legend of this supposed cause-and-effect response has endured in our culture, in part because it accurately portrays how we all occasionally refrain from taking action, often without any regard for the consequences. This tale of the ostrich is aptly similar to how procrastinators respond to situations in real life, because a procrastinator's *learned response* to anxiety over a task is to figuratively bury his head. However, instead of fearing predators, our concern as procrastinators lies with our tasks and our fearful predictions that we will not be able to deal with those tasks effectively.

Of course, we don't literally bury our heads, at least, in the sand. Instead, what we "do" is anything other than the task at hand. In other words, *we avoid*. Our alternative to proper action can be almost anything, so long as it has the ability to absorb our time and attention, relieving us from our concerns and responsibilities. Whichever way you might choose to avoid, it is through the practice of procrastination that one becomes a human ostrich.

We have seen how a procrastinator becomes ruled by in-action. However, it's important to note that at any particular time the average habitual procrastinator has already put off many different tasks that cover a wide spectrum of his needs. Each of these tasks has its own particular life span and because the habitual procrastinator only tends to deal with his tasks when he's forced to by external demands, like deadlines, he acts on a crisis-by-crisis basis, which is an emotionally exhausting way of going about things. Given the fight he's had against taking action, after dealing with a task, he needs a break, which only continues his procrastination. In essence, although he has just put out one fire, the rest of his house continues to smolder; so his break only lasts until the smoke from another fire alerts him of his need to take action once more.

So, as you can see, habitual procrastination is quite complicated in nature. In order to gain more understanding of the human ostrich, let's now take an in-depth look at the characteristics, behaviors, and traits of our newly discovered species.

Chapter Four

The Characteristics, Behaviors, and Traits of the Human Ostrich

HOW WELL DO YOU KNOW yourself? If you identify with the term "habitual procrastinator," or if the procrastination of someone else concerns you, it may prove helpful to take a detailed look at this malady. To change from a habitual procrastinator into a "do"-er not only takes work, but a good deal of patience as well. The material in this chapter will illustrate just how intricately procrastination can seep into a sufferer's life. Let's take an in-depth look into the hows and whys of habitual procrastination, along with its characteristics, behaviors, and traits.

William Shakespeare wrote: "To thine own self be true." What do you think Shakespeare meant by this, and how might it apply to procrastinators? Are procrastinators true to their own selves? My answer to this last question would be a swift and resounding "No." Here's why:

While performing research for this book, I met people on the Internet who identified themselves as procrastinators, and I noticed that they raised one particular concern more than any other. It had less to do with *what* they procrastinated about, and more to do with the anguish, contempt, and even disgust that they had for themselves, culminating in self-hate. Here are two typical comments that I heard:

Student complained:	"I'm always behind on my schoolwork and my room is a mess. Why don't I put more importance on my own stuff?"
Adults remarked:	"If I paid attention to my home the way I handle things at work, I wouldn't come home to this mess. What's wrong with me?"

If you want to change from being a procrastinator, a good starting point would be to make an assessment of the most common aspects of your life in which it could appear.

The 25 Aspects of Procrastination

First, it would be beneficial to identify the traits of habitual procrastinators. While no procrastinator will possess all of the traits listed in the following table, you may find that you recognize or *identify*, with many of them within yourself, or in someone you know. For an in-depth understanding of procrastination, read this section in its entirety. However, if you wish only to read about the traits that you identify with, mark the checkboxes located to the immediate left of each trait listed in this table, and then read the corresponding passages.

❑	1. Many procrastinators believe that worrying over a task is a helpful activity.
❑	2. Charlie says, "I wait until I 'feel like doing it.' It's as if I'm waiting until it feels like 'the right time' before I'll do something. The only thing is, that 'right time' never comes—so nothing gets done."
❑	3. Many procrastinators become overwhelmed by anxiety while trying to choose between several "high priority" tasks.
❑	4. Habitual procrastinators tend to float through life.
❑	5. Habitual procrastinators are resourceful at finding excuses for not doing, and not having done.
❑	6. Many procrastinators report a profound dislike for tasks that are complicated, or take more than a few minutes to accomplish.
❑	7. Some procrastinators find difficulty when they try to alternate between tasks.
❑	8. Many procrastinators find themselves easily distracted from their tasks.
❑	9. Many procrastinators are perfectionists.
❑	10. Quite a few report that they daydream excessively.
❑	11. While doing one task, I wonder, "Should I be doing something else?"
❑	12. Procrastinators worry, "if I 'do,' doesn't that mean that I should always be able to 'do?'"

☐	13. Judith says, "When I complete a large task, I feel like I've earned the right not to 'do' anything for a short while, except—it goes on for too long."
☐	14. Procrastinators feel envy at the "superior abilities" they believe others have.
☐	15. Many procrastinators engage in poor self-communication.
☐	16. Procrastinators suffer from grossly distorted perceptions of time and outcomes, for example: "It'll take 'a thousand years' to get done."
☐	17. A habitual procrastinator's first reaction to a task is usually negative thinking, followed by the belief that any action taken will be fruitless.
☐	18. Many procrastinators suffer from "all-or-nothing thinking."
☐	19. Habitual procrastinators set vague and unreasonable goals.
☐	20. Habitual procrastinators have difficulty planning out their tasks in a logical manner and then following that path until the task's completion.
☐	21. Many procrastinators feel frustrated when they return to an abandoned task.
☐	22. Many feel impatient and frustrated for much of the time.
☐	23. Procrastinators often report that they don't feel satisfied upon a task's completion.
☐	24. Left unresolved, procrastination usually gets worse with time.
☐	25. As procrastination grows stronger—the procrastinator feels weaker!

How many traits of the human ostrich did you identify with? Were you surprised to see some aspects of procrastination that other sufferers have experienced that you haven't? Let's review this list in greater detail:

1. Many Procrastinators Believe That Worrying Over a Task Is a Helpful Activity

I used to believe that by worrying, I was being productive. Instead of planning, I worried. Instead of thinking what I should do next, I worried. And instead of acting, I worried even more. But worrying does not yield results, because it's counter-productive to planning and acting.

In the short term, worrying had its rewards, because when I couldn't do anything else, I could always worry. However, there were times when my worrying spun out of control, so much so, that I became paralyzed with fear at even the thought of dealing with a task. Of course, worrying was actually a substitute for action. So in a certain way, it actually made me feel good to worry, because in spite of filling my mind with anxiety, it felt like I was accomplishing *something*.

There are a few problems with this way of thinking. The first is that worrying is **not** a productive activity. While it may provide you with *something* to do, that *something* is **not** "do"-ing. Secondly, constant worrying can lead to feelings of helplessness and hopelessness. At my own worst, I would actually worry over how much time I was losing to almost ceaseless worrying.

Many procrastinators spend hours at a time lying in bed, wallowing in despair. One procrastinator described these worrying sessions as "listening to my body," as if he were listening for a signal or a cue to say, "take action"; however, that signal never came. I too used to lie awake in bed, while my mind played and replayed scenarios that involved seemingly insurmountable tasks, as though my mind were continuously spinning the dial of a combination lock back and forth in a futile attempt to open the shackle through sheer persistence.

Concurrent with my worrying was an inability to calm down. It was as though my mind could instantly go from relative calm into high-speed anxiety drive, yet it was almost impossible for it to reverse back into calm. In fact, the only way I could stop worrying was to lie down and try to sleep—a sleep that came more from nervous exhaustion than from anything else. As one sufferer put it, "One-half of my brain produces B.S., while the other half buys it."

2. Charlie Says, "I Wait Until I 'Feel Like Doing It.' It's As If I'm Waiting Until It Feels Like 'The Right Time' Before I'll Do Something. The Only Thing Is, That 'Right Time' Never Comes—So Nothing Gets Done."

This characteristic can help define whether someone is a casual or a habitual procrastinator. Remember Stan, the casual procrastinator, and Charlie, the casual habitual procrastinator, from Chapter Two?

Every now and then, Stan intentionally puts off acting on a task while he pursues less urgent things, like taking a nap on a weekend afternoon, or catching a ball game on television. However, if the ball game has been rained out on a Sunday afternoon, that's the time when inspiration strikes him. It's the moment when he asks himself if there's anything he's been putting off. It hardly matters *what* was put off, because as Stan would say, "Now's *the* time." And, even if he doesn't have something in particular to do, Stan will search around his home and find something that needs attention.

Our friend Charlie began putting things off years ago, in the false belief that he was waiting for when things "felt right," because it seemed to follow that if he felt sufficiently inspired, then his results "just had to be better." The only problem with this line of thinking is that Charlie never "feels like" doing much of anything—so the longer that he waits for the "right time" to come along, the longer nothing gets done.

3. Many Procrastinators Become Overwhelmed by Anxiety While Trying to Choose Between Several "High Priority" Tasks

At any given time the average habitual procrastinator typically has several tasks that he has put off which usually comprise a mix of high-priority tasks and intermediate-level or less urgent tasks. One such procrastinator is Jerry, who has a large assortment of tasks requiring attention.

When asked to identify the one task that was clearly his highest priority, Jerry mentioned that his car's inspection sticker would expire in a few days' time. Then, without missing a beat, he added that the reason why he hadn't dealt with it was because other high-priority tasks had prevented him. You see, Jerry's apartment was a complete mess, and then his old high school buddy Matt, who lives in Canada, had unexpectedly called with news that he and his girlfriend Cathy were about to take a long-distance drive. Matt wondered if they could stay overnight at Jerry's place, which was tomorrow. Suddenly, housecleaning had jumped from somewhere near the bottom of Jerry's mental "to-do list" to "high-priority." Jerry seethed in self-anger for allowing himself to wind up in this situation "for the zillionth time," and complained that he "kept getting himself into the same old situations, but with different people each time."

Since he'd never take action unless he were forced to, only external circumstances prompted Jerry into acting; however, by continually working on a crisis-by-crisis basis, Jerry builds up a great deal of self-directed anger, which plays havoc with his ability to view his tasks with clarity. Where a non-procrastinator would deem Jerry's lifestyle as far too stressful, as far as Jerry is concerned, "it's just another day." As a result of his ever-changing priorities, Jerry is floating through life; putting out one fire after another, without ever getting control of the conflagration. This brings us to our next characteristic of the human ostrich.

4. Habitual Procrastinators Tend to Float Through Life

By acting only when his hand is forced by circumstances, and not through his own decisions, Jerry refuses to take responsibility for his own life. He often says that he "doesn't like being tied down to anything," and it shows.

Having never quite *found himself* in the workplace, Jerry has held a seemingly endless variety of jobs, and he's switched careers several times as well. He's also picked up and moved a few times, almost hoping that by changing location, his life too might change.

By not attaching himself to any particular vocation or location, Jerry has enjoyed a certain sense of freedom—but he's now seeing a cost to this lifestyle. He has begun to feel envious of friends whose lives appear more stable and established than his own.

5. Habitual Procrastinators Are Resourceful at Finding Excuses for Not Doing, and Not Having Done

The only thing that could possibly be greater than the number of tasks a habitual procrastinator has put off might be the number of excuses they can come up with. In a sense, it comes down to what they're most skilled at: "doing," or "not doing." Which one describes you best?

If you said "not-doing," try not to be hard on yourself. Few persons would take the time to read this book unless they had a genuine problem with procrastination. It's better to be honest with yourself about the extent of your habitual procrastination than to continue making excuses for your in-actions, as well as excuses for your excuses.

Excuses were an important mechanism to the way in which I procrastinated. In essence, they provided me with a back-up system to bolster what little self-esteem I had. While some excuses worked really well—others simply worked. Without a bona fide excuse, what else could you possibly say to a superior at work who was expecting a report that had not been submitted on time? How about: "It seemed boring to me at the time; do you *still* want it?" That just doesn't have the air of authority that "I was too busy to get around to it" has.

6. Many Procrastinators Report A Profound Dislike for Tasks That Are Complicated, or Take More Than a Few Minutes to Accomplish

Marching in step along with not "do"-ing is the procrastinator's desire for all tasks to be simple in nature, and to flow effortlessly toward completion. The procrastinator does not stand alone in this respect. He shares similar attitudes with compulsive gamblers who want to "take the easy way out," and those who seek the equivalent in *get-rich-quick schemes*, which purport to offer the benefits of hard work, but without the responsibilities and all the hassles.

Gambling also describes how procrastinators lead their lives, because they are playing the odds that they will succeed in *getting over* on their responsibilities. While we might hope that by diverting our attention away from pressing matters, we'll regain some sense of control over our lives, although we may not be gambling in a casino, our long-term results are similar. While the gambler loses money, we lose pride within ourselves.

It's natural for habitual procrastinators to feel overwhelmed; and to want to avoid, or to flee when faced with a complicated task. Avoidance goes hand in hand with frustration—the more frustrated we feel, the more we may delay dealing with our tasks. This is one reason why many procrastinators begin to *shut down* at just the thought of dealing with a complicated task.

If it's been a long while since you've dealt with a complicated task, it's important to understand that it's only natural to feel apprehensive towards changing your approach towards "do"-ing; but keep in mind that we're not at the point where we're ready to deal with any of that. In Section Two of this book, you will learn how to begin taking small steps at changing long-held habits. For now, we only want to continue observing the behaviors of the human ostrich.

7. Some Procrastinators Find Difficulty When They Try to Alternate Between Tasks

Almost all habitual procrastinators occasionally surprise themselves by acting on a task. However, because they've usually been forced to act by a deadline or by an unsympathetic superior, their actions tend to be less planned out, and often more of a direct approach. Moments before taking action, a habitual procrastinator's attitude is quite similar to an Army battalion taking a hill in a "now or never," "do—or die!" effort.

Once they've begun, many procrastinators are so determined to plow through and finish their task, they may rebuff the attempts of others to change from what they're engaged in. *"Don't try to stop me, I'm on a roll!"* Karen excitedly says to a co-worker with her head buried in a pile of papers. While Karen thinks, "When my back's up against a wall, that's when I get it done," her co-workers tell quite a different tale: "Karen's always late with her reports. Heaven help anyone who asks her to switch tasks when her paperwork is late."

Karen's dilemma is she can't switch from one task to another. She's so used to putting things off that she only sees herself capable of either half-hearted attempts, or whole-hearted all-out attacks on her tasks—*"No matter what!"* Karen even calls this her "winning combo": "Put something off for as long as you possibly can, until you can't put it off any longer. Then, take action!"

It wasn't all that long ago that, like Karen, I would have found switching between tasks nearly impossible. Today I can break a project into parts and work on one, or stop and switch to another part of the same task, or temporarily leave it altogether to work on something else entirely. Without getting caught up in the hows and whys, just for now, understand that change within yourself is possible.

8. Many Procrastinators Find Themselves Easily Distracted from Their Tasks

Keeping one's nose to the grindstone and focusing on a task tends to be a challenge for many procrastinators. It seems as if our very nature were to shy away from our tasks. Just as two magnets with like poles repel from each other, procrastinators tend to automatically shrink from their tasks.

Why are we like this? Well, why shouldn't we be? After all, we procrastinators have been perfecting "the art of avoidance" for years, and if you practice just about anything long enough, you're bound to become good at it.

When I attended college, I found that my math skills were rusty, so I went to the "math lab" for a brush up. I can recall watching the lab's volunteer tutor, an elderly gentleman who had the patience of a saint. He would go through a math example with a student slowly and carefully, and I would watch from a short distance, waiting to see if he showed frustration at a student's difficulty with a math problem, but quite the opposite was true. Instead of rushing things, this gentleman would work step-by-step with a student, and at that student's pace.

While watching this gentleman that day, I felt a bit of discomfort. It seemed as though he had *something* I hadn't, and that something was **patience**. It may well be that the impact and the resulting memory of that day so long ago indicates just how in need of patience I was at the time. If only I had learned that lesson back then.

If you find difficulty staying on track and keeping focused, you can train yourself to stick with a task by developing patience from within. If there's one thing that I know now, it's that **"the enemy of procrastination is patience."** Keep that filed somewhere in the back of your mind; I have a strong feeling that we'll be coming back to it later.

9. Many Procrastinators Are Perfectionists

Perfectionism, as it relates to procrastination, is the need to have everything proper before taking action. While there's nothing wrong with planning and preparing for action, if you can't get past those initial stages, then you'll almost certainly get stuck in the mud and muck of procrastination. For example, a perfectionist might say, "Why ruin the opportunity to do an outstanding job, when the outcome could be ruined in the haste of rushing?" This leads us back to the need of developing patience from within in order to have the mental strength to focus on and then deal with our tasks.

Perfectionism often comes disguised as "making a smart move" through the withholding of action in order to prepare for any and all circumstances; however, it can also prevent us from taking action, such as when a prior requirement must be fulfilled in order to act on a task. For example, Fred won't have a guest over to his place unless it's absolutely *spotless*, but spotless is a relatively rare condition for his living space to be in, so much so that it prevents him from looking for a girlfriend. However, as long as Fred's place doesn't look *perfect*, he won't have guests over. You might think that with this condition Fred would spend practically all of his free time cleaning up his place—yet he never finds the time to clean and he's never in the mood to clean either, so his procrastination continues unabated.

10. Quite a Few Report That They Daydream Excessively

Remember that lecture I gave at the Stress Relief Club of Stuyvesant High School? While I was there, I asked the students to share some of the ways that they've procrastinated. "I daydream a lot." replied one student. That student deserves an "A" for honesty.

The truth is that we all daydream from time to time; however, some of us do it a lot more than others. So, where does one draw the line between a pleasant diversion, and something that gets in the way? While it's natural to tear yourself away from everyday life, even if it's only in your head, some people procrastinate by engaging in daydreaming to such an extent that it can add up to a significant amount of time spent during an average day.

When a person decides to change something in his or her life, whether it's going back to school, joining a gym, or reducing the amount of time he or she spends procrastinating, that person seeks to transform him or herself. As you start your journey toward changing away from the habit of procrastination, it's important to keep an open mind in order to discover which characteristics you incorporate into your present procrastination.

11. While Doing One Task, I Wonder, "Should I Be Doing Something Else?"

"Damned if I do, damned if I don't, and damned if I do something else." This seems to be the habitual procrastinator's mantra. As previously mentioned, many of us experience difficulty staying on track until a task's completion. One of the ways we engage in distracting ourselves from a task is by second-guessing ourselves with statements like, "There are more important things that I need to be working on right now."

When we do this, we cause doubt to grow in our minds, and we are then apt to put a halt to our work by picking up another task. Suppose for a moment that we changed tasks because our second task was indeed more important than the original task we were working on. All we'd need to do then would be to act on the second task until its completion, and then return to our original task.

However, that's not how habitual procrastinators act. Instead, after putting aside our original task and then commencing work on our second task, we would then doubt ourselves again with something along the lines of, "How can I work on this when I've got other things that need my attention?" Then, we would repeat that same behavior. It's through this behavioral cycle whereby nothing is accomplished. The solution to this is learning how to prioritize by becoming comfortable with your decisions, and then focusing your attention on just one task until its completion. This will be discussed in detail in Section Two.

12. Procrastinators Worry, "If I 'Do,' Doesn't That Mean That I Should Always Be Able to 'Do?'"

Another way habitual procrastinators distract themselves is by worrying that were they to find the courage to tackle a difficult task, that would then prove they had the ability to do it all along, which would then instantly obligate them to "do" everything that they had been putting off. It's through this way of thinking that a habitual procrastinator will put himself on trial and then act as his own judge, jury, and prosecutor.

If you identify with this aspect of procrastination, remember that all anyone can do is one thing at a time. Even if other people pride themselves on being multi-taskers, while they may have the ability to juggle several tasks for a short while, they can only work on one of them at any one time. Try not to concern yourself with the worry that one day you'll suddenly be cured of procrastination, and then be obligated to work non-stop to clear up many years worth of unpleasant tasks. Nothing could be further from the truth.

A person changes from being a habitual procrastinator slowly, and over a good length of time. That's one reason why this book is not called "Beat Procrastination in 30 Days!" Instant change doesn't usually happen, and you are probably not going to turn into the world's newest superhero who fights delay, disorder, and untidiness throughout the planet. We make substantial and effective changes in our lives by going through a process, and you will learn that process as you read this book and then implement changes into your life. If you find yourself fraught with worry over your future as a recovering procrastinator, you may find it helpful to come back to this paragraph and re-read it a few times.

13. Judith Says, "When I Complete a Large Task, I Feel Like I've Earned the Right Not to 'Do' Anything for a Short While, Except—It Goes On for Too Long."

Many procrastinators are capable of tremendous activity when special circumstances are involved. "I'll just die if Mom and Dad see my place like this. I only have two days to whip this place into shape," says Judith. True to her word, two days later her apartment is not only shipshape, but it can also withstand her mother's infamous white-glove test. Judith's parents leave a few days later, and ever so slowly, the neatness she created begins to unravel. "That which I can create, I too can destroy," Judith half-jokingly says to herself. Oddly enough, while she doesn't really want the neatness of her place to come apart, "it just does."

Judith doesn't see herself as a procrastinator, but as someone who "gets back at her responsibilities." Instead of seeing housecleaning as something that can be done periodically, the only way she knows how to go about it is by launching all-out assaults. Judith expends a great deal of energy over a very short timeframe, so much so that she not only exhausts herself, but she also builds up resentments against housecleaning, or whatever other task she deals with in this sort of manner. She puts an end to any future housecleaning unless, once again, special circumstances dictate that it must be done.

What Judith fails to see is that it's far easier to do a little cleaning every now and then, than it is to accomplish several years' worth of cleaning in the space of only a few days. Although it's admirable that she's able to work straight through until her apartment is *clean enough*, her life would probably be easier if she knew how to "do" in smaller chunks. In addition, while she worries about her mother's "white glove test," she doesn't have the courage to tell her mother that her apartment needs only to be *clean enough* for Judith alone. If you find that you deal with tasks in the same fashion as Judith, you may wish to endeavor on learning how to become satisfied in doing small amounts of work over a longer period of time.

14. Procrastinators Feel Envy at the "Superior Abilities" They Believe Others Have

Procrastination causes us to feel two types of effects: while there is the short-term joy that comes from getting over on one's tasks, there's also the glum outlook upon life that develops as a result of losing trust in one's ability to care for oneself. Just like seeing our distorted reflection in a funhouse mirror, we may begin seeing others as more capable than ourselves; and worse, we might then begin to look down upon ourselves. Consequently, we become poster-children for low self-esteem.

Earlier on, we compared Stan and Charlie, a casual and a habitual procrastinator, respectively. What especially frustrates Charlie is the fact that while he has about as much time to deal with his tasks as anyone else, he winds up getting little, if anything, accomplished. Not only does Charlie envy the abilities of someone like Stan to get things done, what really confounds Charlie is Stan's ability to simply *start acting*.

As I worked at overcoming my difficulties with habitual procrastination, I began to feel better about myself. In time, I even developed a bit of self-confidence, which made me feel a lot less concerned about how *others* supposedly were "do"-ing.

15. Many Procrastinators Engage in Poor Self-Communication

Just as our thoughts dictate our actions, they can also deter us from undertaking action. Many habitual procrastinators have an almost constant, negative internal dialogue buzzing through their brains, which is the result of second-guessing themselves, or otherwise putting themselves down. Some procrastinators have reported that their negative chatter runs off and on from awakening until bedtime.

Most habitual procrastinators only hear their negative self-dialogue, which convincingly warns them of the dangers lurking in the shadows, with statements like:

➢ "It's too complicated!"
➢ "This is boring!"
➢ "I'd really rather be doing something else."
➢ "I'm not up to dealing with this."

Interestingly, while procrastinators tend only listen to their negative self-statements, which concern the supposed consequences of taking action, they fail to consider the consequences of not acting—which leads to poor decision-making and even poorer outcomes.

Why is it that procrastinators think this way? Part of the rationale of this thinking is that procrastinators do not generate positive outcomes with any great frequency, because all they're used to considering are the potential risks that might, or might not, come about from taking action. So, with his mindset permanently switched to the "don't act" position, the habitual procrastinator deals with life by continually suffering through his decisions and responsibilities.

16. Procrastinators Suffer from Grossly Distorted Perceptions of Time and Outcomes, for Example: "It'll Take 'A Thousand Years' to Get Done."

There's an old adage concerning optimism and pessimism that asks: "Would you view a drinking glass as half-full, or half-empty?" However, a habitual procrastinator's response is more likely to be: "I never get a full glass of water." What does that tell you about how a habitual procrastinator thinks?

What this response shows us is that many procrastinators also suffer from an exaggerated form of anticipatory distress, or, what we might call, "fear of the future." It's a concern, as well as a prediction, that they'll incur horrible results just for getting involved in a task or a project. As a result of this thinking, they prefer to sit things out. Here are just some of the ways in which habitual procrastinators can magnify their concerns:

➢ The procrastinator is greatly concerned over negative results that haven't yet come about, as the result of actions that have yet to be taken.

> ➤ He imagines calamities and worries more about the images that he sees in his head, rather than concerning himself with the all too real consequences that could arise from not taking action.

> ➤ The procrastinator worries that he will suffer shame and embarrassment from the opinions, comments, criticism, or invalidation of others. "Why try? I'm only going to get shot down for it, anyway!"

> ➤ The procrastinator fears that accomplishments will lead to new choices, new decisions, new expectations, and more obligations.

> ➤ Being generally pessimistic, procrastinators often worry that after taking action, that they will be disappointed with their results. Although a non-procrastinator would readily see the falsehood of this line of thinking, it makes perfect sense to the procrastinator, because if you haven't accomplished anything for a long while, you don't have any hard evidence with which to prove that acting often results in favorable outcomes. In short, the procrastinator believes that any action on his part will probably not yield a positive outcome. This particular characteristic of habitual procrastination will be dealt with in greater detail in the next section of this chapter.

If you are at the point where it seems as though "everything takes forever," remember that although this may seem true, this is only a feeling, and *feelings are not facts.* For now, try not to overwhelm yourself with worry over how capable or incapable you may or may not be; after all, we can all stand some improvement in our own lives. All we want to do right now is continue observing the characteristics and behaviors of the human ostrich, in order to gain a better perspective of how procrastination has the ability to affect us.

17. A Habitual Procrastinator's First Reaction to a Task Is Usually Negative Thinking, Followed by the Belief That Any Action Taken Will Be Fruitless

Doom and gloom fill the minds of many habitual procrastinators. Plans are vague, goals are unattainable, and results seem uncontrollable. When it comes to our tasks, we not only start off on a sour note, but we also amplify the negative.

For example, when faced with the task of mopping the living room floor after accidentally spilling food, my internal negative chatter would run all the way from a terribly derogatory self-statement, to the convoluted logic of "Why did I even bother?" Here's how that internal conversation went:

➢ "I'm such an idiot for spilling that."
➢ "I hate mopping."
➢ "How long is this going to take?"
➢ "Am I mopping correctly?"
➢ "What if the stain is still there afterwards?"
➢ "It's no use—it's not going to make a difference." "It's almost all gone, but I don't think I can get it one hundred percent clean."
➢ And finally: "Other people may think the floor is clean, but I'll know what happened."

Habitual procrastination led me into habitual worrying, and that led me towards having a negative outlook upon life. Oddly enough, my negative outlook served as a protective measure of sorts, saving my feelings from disappointment and discouragement, because no matter what the outcome might be, I had never expected a positive outcome in the first place.

You may be anxious to end your procrastinating ways, but please remember to go easy on yourself. It's of crucial importance to know that change comes gradually, and to remember that procrastination's enemy is patience. To attempt one swift try at changing what has likely been nearly a lifelong habit will almost certainly have very poor results, along with a good deal of negative self-talk along the lines of "I knew I couldn't do it!" Changing one's behavior involves a process: one of learning, trying, relearning, and retrying. Take my advice: "slow down and start enjoying the scenery." Aim for a long-lasting difference in your life.

18. Many Procrastinators Suffer from "All-Or-Nothing Thinking"

When a habitual procrastinator faces a task, he often looks at it as though he was starting a journey across a vast expanse without the aid of a map. Like someone who only knows their starting point (his undone task) and final destination (completion of his task), he may feel overwhelmed because while he has an idea of what he wants to accomplish, he doesn't know which route to take towards completing it.

Faced with a formidable challenge, he may search for a starting point, but he finds that all he's able to tell himself is, "C'mon, do it! Let's go! Try!" This is a good strategy if you're sitting in the bleachers at a sporting event and you're cheering your team on—but when you direct that same energy toward yourself and don't take action, that energy does nothing except to build up upon itself. Eventually, it returns to you in feelings of frustration, resentment, and shame. Feeling lost in a sea of emotions, the procrastinator stops all action: "Why try? I just can't do it!"

If someone goes through this often enough, he may wind up doing only those tasks that require the least amount of effort, or things that can be completed in only one attempt. This helps explain why many habitual procrastinators find themselves puzzled when tasks that formerly took a reasonable amount of time and energy to complete, like paying bills or balancing the checkbook, are now emotionally draining. The reason for this is, as the habit of procrastination becomes stronger, the habitual procrastinator's self-confidence grows weaker. Left unchecked, this can grow to the extent where, if a task can't be completed in one attempt, the procrastinator then feels that there's no point in even trying.

19. Habitual Procrastinators Set Vague and Unreasonable Goals

Planning and preparation are two key areas where habitual procrastinators occasionally drop the ball. Many procrastinators complain they don't have enough time to plan, but this is usually due to the last-minute nature of their lives. Concerned by the possibility of encountering a negative outcome, they find that the act of planning provokes anxiety within themselves, because with planning comes responsibility for the outcome of the task. An additional concern encountered while planning is that if the wrong strategy were chosen, it might confirm one of a procrastinator's worst fears, that he's "incapable." It's for this reason that many procrastinators try to *wing it*, or "do" without planning.

Although a procrastinator may gain a sense of freedom from winging it, underlying this freedom is the fear that if his plans backfire, they could wind up working against him. To prevent this, he sets vague and unrealistic goals that by their very nature do not include clearly defined strategies.

Much like the example in the previous section of taking a road trip without a map or any other type of navigational aid, *when you fail to plan, you plan to fail.*

20. Habitual Procrastinators Have Difficulty Planning Out Their Tasks in a Logical Manner and Then Following That Path Until the Task's Completion

In the previous section, we saw how habitual procrastinators set vague and unreasonable goals for themselves, and that many of them don't like the hassle of plans, hoping instead to *wing it* and *be done with it.* As a habitual procrastinator, I too acted in this way, because I had linked the concept of "planning" to "the burden of responsibility." I believed that if I made plans and something went wrong, that I would be held responsible for the outcome; and responsibility wasn't something that I was too keen in taking on. Today, I can see that this was simply a cover-up for the lack of a crucial skill on my part, that of *logical planning.* Without knowing how to logically plan things, although I occasionally accomplished some tasks, I usually did them in an inefficient way.

That's not to say I never planned out a task, there were many times when I did; however, although I may have conceived of the steps needed to complete a task, more often than not I would divert from those plans. The usual cause for my detours was because, sometime after starting out on the task, I would discover that one or two of the steps were either boring or were terribly complicated. Then, instead of sticking to the plan or devising some new steps, I would jump ahead to a step that seemed more appealing.

Of course, I'd eventually need to go back to whichever boring steps I had skipped, which I'd attempt to rush through as quickly as I could. Unfortunately, this strategy worked against me, because the steps I had put off were the ones that required a bit of extra effort. Instead of giving them the time they needed, I rushed through them, which is not exactly a good strategy for accomplishment. Afterwards, I was left with an unpleasant memory of how I had gone about dealing with that task, mostly because of how I had mishandled those difficult steps. So, even if things had gone relatively well up until the point where I went off-course, my most recent memory of the experience was of feeling overwhelmed, which wasn't the best motivation for my future tasks.

Today, logical planning is a regular part of the preparations that I undertake before acting on a task. In addition, I now know that part of the reason behind my not wanting to deal with steps that were complicated or tedious was because my own impatience often got the better of me.

21. Many Procrastinators Feel Frustrated When They Return to an Abandoned Task

In the last few sections of this chapter, we've looked at some of the negative thinking patterns many procrastinators have. When these patterns work in conjunction with each other, procrastination can become a habit that can eventually grow to the point where the procrastinator sees himself as less than an adult, while at the same time, his tasks seem almost to overshadow him, as though they've become larger than life. With all this in our way, it might seem impossible for us to accomplish any of the older tasks that we had long abandoned; however, there are some conditions when we will deal with them, such as when we'll pay our electric bill to avoid having the lights shut off.

When a habitual procrastinator puts off a task, it's often because he has told himself, "I can't do it," and the more he thinks that, the more he believes it. Just as the more often you do something, the more likely it is to become a habit, the more often that you put a task aside, the less likely it is that you will want to deal with it. If this continues, it becomes easier and easier to keep on *not dealing* with it, than to otherwise face it. For this reason, returning to a task can easily escalate into a conflicting ordeal, because the tasks that we allow to linger can often begin to take on a power of their own. In other words, the longer that we put off a task, and the more false starts we attempt, the more *internal resistance* we'll feel towards that task. Electrical engineers have a word for a form of internal resistance—they call it "reluctance," which, coincidentally, fits habitual procrastinators to a tee.

22. Many Feel Impatient and Frustrated for Much of the Time

If any single characteristic or trait of habitual procrastination has led to feelings of frustration and bewilderment, impatience is *it*, because it causes its sufferers to feel as if "there's never enough time to get things done." While one might believe that this phenomenon is caused by today's faster pace of life, over two hundred years ago the British poet Edward Young wrote, "Procrastination is the thief of time."

Impatience led me to believe that no result would be good enough, and that the results of anything I did would always be second-rate. At the same time, I also believed that by doing nothing I was protesting my situation, like a lone wolf of sorts, fighting authority and responsibility. However, the truth is that I was only prolonging my own agony.

23. Procrastinators Often Report That They Don't Feel Satisfied Upon a Task's Completion

As previously mentioned, even the worst procrastinator occasionally completes a task, if only because he's been forced into action by the potential consequences of the situation. With little serving as motivation except the threat of penalty following completion of a task, how does the procrastinator feel, and what does he tell himself? Does he grasp the bathroom sink with both hands and say to his own reflection in the mirror, "You did it! I always knew you could!" Or does he try to avoid his reflection, and if so, what do you think he tells himself then?

One of the peculiarities of habitual procrastination is the "I just can't win" factor. After all, if you believe that most every task will be fraught with agony and will produce dismal results, then why even try? Why is it that habitual procrastinators often feel this way? One possible reason is that we have developed an unreasonable expectation that we should feel satisfied and content for most, if not all, of the time. Boredom and struggle do not fit in with an otherwise idyllic and carefree life. However, while we would all like to bask in the warm glow of feeling satisfied for most of the time, if we make this a pre-condition or expectation, we run the risk of occasionally being let down by a certain force, most commonly know as: *reality.*

So, the only way that anyone can remain in such a false reality is by steadfastly refusing to deal with the unpleasant or difficult tasks that come our way. If we continually avoid our tasks because we've lost our sense of accomplishment, then it's only natural that when we're faced with a new task, instead of dealing with it, we'll most likely procrastinate.

24. Left Unresolved, Procrastination Usually Gets Worse With Time

Similar to other disorders that can grow in scope with the passage of time, such as phobias and addictions, procrastination can also intrude into one's life, sometimes in unexpected ways. For example, "routine housekeeping" begins to lose meaning when the word "routine" is used less and less in actual practice. Over time, the procrastinator may become so disconnected from routine tasks, that little if anything gets done on a scheduled or "routine" basis. Household cleaning that might have been done regularly in the past falls by the wayside, and now gets done only on an as-needed basis, if it's done at all. Over time, the procrastinator finds himself overwhelmed by all the tasks that require his attention, and he copes in the only manner he knows—he takes on his problems on a "crisis-by-crisis" basis, often as a result of external deadlines or from the prospect of uncomfortable, if not unbearable consequences.

As the habitual procrastinator withdraws further from "routine" activities, he may develop additional measures that will assist in keeping him in the land of non-"do"-ers. For example: Henry only cleans his apartment when it's absolutely necessary to do so, like when guests are visiting. Afterwards, Henry not only allows his apartment to become messy again, but he decides that having visitors over isn't really worth all the effort that cleaning takes. In addition, deciding to stop having people over eliminates the chore and responsibility of regular housekeeping. Unfortunately for Henry, he then pays for this decision by becoming somewhat of a hermit.

Even worse, Henry's single, and he's not only lonely, but he occasionally wonders if he were to start dating again, how he could ever invite a woman over. Perhaps she might not return after a first visit. Suppose she made a comment or even laughed at the sight of his place. Unbearable to bear the thought of being laughed at by a love interest, Henry tries to forget about dating by trying to convince himself that he's too old, and that he's *missed the boat*. If all that weren't bad enough, Henry's also concerned that if a pipe were to burst in his apartment, would the plumber report him to his landlord?

At this point, with what appear to be too many tasks to accomplish, and, believing that he doesn't have enough time to do a good enough job on each of them to justify taking action, Henry finds himself hopelessly stuck. Even if Henry wanted to give himself a fresh start, it's likely that he doesn't know how to arrange going about his tasks in an orderly fashion; and because of this, Henry's become accustomed to acting impulsively. Not coincidentally, his results are often less than desirable. Then, after Henry completes a task by cutting corners, he berates himself with negative self-talk, sometimes even calling himself "stupid," which lowers his already plummeting self-worth and self-esteem. However, Henry isn't "stupid"; he's simply fallen into a mental pit because he doesn't know any other way of life.

Henry only knows leaving home for work each day and coming straight back to what he jokingly refers to as "The National Junk Preserve." Instead of working on his tasks the moment that he returns home from work, he turns his television on to distract himself from the squalor and loneliness that he finds himself in. In short, Henry feels helpless and hopeless.

25. As Procrastination Grows Stronger—The Procrastinator Feels Weaker!

Here's a riddle: "How many sides does a barrel have?" The answer is two: an outside, and an inside. Now, here's another riddle: "How many sides does a habitual procrastinator have?" The answer is the same, two—but in this case they consist of the outer-selves that we display to the world, and our inner-selves which we hide from view.

There are times when we can surprise ourselves with our ability to conceal our inner-self. One such time for me was when I went to job interviews, where the name of the game was to look *eager* for work. That was quite an accomplishment indeed, for if only the interviewer could have seen my quivering insides. In search of an administrative position, one of the attributes listed on my résumé was "neat and organized." Luckily for me a home inspection wasn't part of the interview process—for if one were required, I would never have gotten the job.

However, little did I know at the time, that the condition of my apartment actually did have an affect on how I did on job interviews, because I constantly carried the burden of feeling like an ineffective adult—and the worse my apartment was, the weaker I felt. So, while singing my outer-self's praises to the interviewer, I'm sure my body language gave away my inner-self's conflict.

Did you see yourself reflected in any of The 25 Aspects of Procrastination? If so, did you check off a few items on the list, but found later on that you identified with more of them? For many habitual procrastinators, the following narrative seems to practically sum up our condition:

"I should pay those bills, now…
"But I still don't want to…
"I have a little time before they're due…
"I know I should pay them…
"But I just don't feel like it right now….
"I don't know why on earth I'm like this…
"No one else I know does this…
"What's wrong with me?"

Habitual procrastination causes its sufferers to feel like they're *less than* other persons, and it makes them feel sad, aimless, and unfulfilled in their lives. They also feel impatient and frustrated for much of the time, as though "there isn't enough time" and "they'll never be enough time" to do all the things that they need to do, yet simultaneously, don't want to deal with. Feeling helpless and hopeless for much of the time, is it any surprise if habitual procrastinators complain that they sometimes feel depressed?

Chapter Five

Procrastination and Depression

I N THE LAST CHAPTER WE saw that when habitual procrastination is allowed to grow unchecked, it can overtake its victims. As a result of an ever-mounting number of undone tasks, the procrastinator may feel guilty for his self-inflicted predicaments, and overwhelmed by his emotions, which can combine to the point where he feels helpless and hopeless. When someone finds himself in this situation, it's almost certain that he will feel miserable.

One procrastinator remarked that he knew he'd crossed the line one morning when his in-actions had progressed to the point where he found himself unable to leave home for work. Here's how he described that event:

➢ "I disliked doing the laundry, who doesn't? I mean, can you name one person that actually likes doing laundry? Not just because it's boring, but because it just feels like a complete waste of time. I'd rather be doing other things, anything else, but the laundry.
➢ "I got to the point where I would only do the wash when I saw that I was beginning to run out of clean clothes.
➢ "Then one day, I had no clean underwear, absolutely none. I wound up bent over my hamper picking through everything, trying to find the cleanest-looking dirty item. Finding one, I gave it a good couple of shakes to air it out. I don't know if anyone at work noticed anything peculiar that day, but I was disgusted with myself."

Although the butt of jokes for time immemorial, the life of a long-term procrastinator is filled with self-disgust and suffering over lost opportunities. Although I am not a medical doctor, I have lived the life of a long-term habitual procrastinator and from what I've discovered in bringing this book to fruition—I think it's fair to say, "Show me a habitual procrastinator, and I'll show you a person who probably suffers from depression."

Which Came First—Procrastination or Depression?

Imagine a person who only takes care of his responsibilities when he's forced to. Although he has sufficient funds in his checking account, he doesn't pay his bills until further delay would mean incurring financial penalties, the loss of his electricity, telephone, or cable television, and the possibility that his credit rating could be affected. Try to picture this person in your mind. How would he describe himself to someone else? Do you think he would call himself a "take-charge" individual? Do you think he would be in good spirits, or might he feel low? What would he look like? Would he look cheerful and in control, or might he cast his head down—as though perpetually gazing at his shoes?

I know how habitual procrastination caused me to behave and to feel. I seemed capable of doing anything I put my mind to, so long as it was in the pursuit of avoiding my tasks. In order to avoid reality, I would "do" practically anything—except deal with whatever task really needed my attention. So, the things I wound up "do"-ing were the things that didn't matter in the long-term—like watching television or oversleeping. Meanwhile, the fewer tasks I dealt with, the larger my "to-do" list grew.

As that list grew larger and larger, I began feeling as though I bore the weight of the world on my shoulders. Avoidance and anxiety ruled the roost, and while my "to-do" list might have contained only a few complicated tasks, the majority of it was comprised of less important tasks. In my haste to avoid feeling overwhelmed by the tasks that I wanted to avoid, I wound up avoiding the entire list—so *nothing* that needed "do"-ing ever got done. My "to-do" list seemed almost larger than life, and every time I reminded myself that I should deal with something on it, all I could think about were all the times I'd turned away from it. It seemed that for every time I had accomplished something on my "to-do" list, there had been a hundred times when I had picked it up, looked it over, put it down again, and walked away from it. As that list came to control my life, in turn, it left me feeling less and less capable.

As time passed, my "to-do" list became a "things I hadn't done" list. That list didn't exist exclusively on paper, because I constantly carried it around in my mind, which made me feel bogged down. Every time I thought of it, it reminded me of just how ineffective I was, which caused me to think poorly about myself. Sometimes in frustration, I would tear up an old list and start a new one, but this only provided temporary relief. In short, I was fit to be tied, frustrated, down on myself, and felt unable to tackle just about anything.

Even other people's encouragement didn't help. I once had a girlfriend who had a favorite expression. In a true Brooklyn accent, she would say, "Hey, don't sweat the small stuff!" I can only guess that she kept saying this to me because I was in the midst of a depression and this was her way of trying to help. One day I was talking with her about all of the things I needed to do when again she remarked, "Hey, don't sweat the small stuff!" I then thought about all of the things I'd been putting off that made me feel overwhelmed. I needed to buy stamps, I needed to buy milk, I needed to mop my apartment's floors, I needed to deposit my paycheck, and I needed to watch two television programs that I had recorded. I needed…, I needed…, I needed all of it to go away. I turned to her and said, "It's all small stuff! Everything I need to do is small stuff—and I can't do it!"

Somewhere along the line, I had forgotten how to take care of my needs. I had lost my motivation and habitual procrastination had become a way of life. Simple tasks were tremendous burdens, complicated tasks seemed impossible to deal with, and I only dealt with tasks when I faced the threat of severe penalties, or because other people or institutions required me to act. There seemed to be little true pleasure in my life: only obligations and the avoidance of them. So, which came first—procrastination, or depression? Did my procrastination cause me to become depressed, or did depression cause me to procrastinate? I believe that both fed each another—so no matter which came first, it was quite easy to tell what would come next.

The High Cost of Free Time

Looking back, it is any wonder that I spent much of my free time watching television or sleeping a day away? These scenarios occurred more times than I can count—here's how they usually played themselves out:

After watching television on my couch, I would start dozing off. Eventually, I would position myself to where I was lying across the couch, however, with my head uncomfortably propped against the couch's armrest. After 20 or 30 minutes asleep, I'd begin feel an annoying pain in my neck; but having lost the plot of whatever I'd been watching, I would tell myself: "If you're going to sleep—then sleep!" and I'd stumble off to the bedroom, awakening some ninety minutes later. By then, the afternoon sky had turned dark, and I would think, "What's wrong with me? I had time to get stuff done, and I've wasted it! How could I be *so dumb?*"

Still, did I ever react to one of these all too frequent emotional downturns by springing into action to make up for lost time? No. Instead, I wallowed in my depression. Quite sick of myself, yet not knowing a different way of responding, I did the only thing I was really good at—I continued avoiding my tasks while now attempting to avoid the bad feelings that had come about from having fallen asleep on my couch. How I continued that avoidance depended on what I was up for.

On some nights I would pig out on Chinese food with a fat-laden dish practically guaranteed to fill me up and put me straight to bed, like sesame chicken on a bed of pork fried rice. On other evenings, I'd draw my window shades, shut the room lights, turn my TV on while keeping the sound off, and smoke marijuana while playing a favorite CD, enjoying my own multimedia experience. It was my own little world, a home away from home—at home. All because I needed to escape the feelings that plagued me, the feelings that led me into depression.

Could the Symptoms of Depression be a Sign of Something Else?

Let's say that a person who was feeling poorly visited his physician one day and complained of having a lack of energy and an inability to finish projects, as well as feeling reluctant about taking on new tasks. What do you think the doctor might surmise as the cause of this patient's condition? Although the physician would probably take the patient's complete medical history and order blood tests in order to rule out any biological causes for the patient's lethargy, the physician might also suspect mental depression. This would be no surprise because loss of interest in normal everyday activities is a common symptom of depression. However, from first-hand experience, it is my belief that procrastination isn't merely a symptom of depression, but that in some individuals, procrastination can actually cause depression.

Depression is diagnosed based on symptoms the patient presents to the doctor, just as a heart attack might be diagnosed based on symptoms of a crushing sensation atop the chest and an acute pain shooting down the left arm. The symptoms, along with the doctor's training, dictate the course of treatment. In the case of depression, the diagnosis is almost always followed with a prescription for a medication, along with a referral for psychotherapy. This is the usual treatment for the average person who finds himself in this situation. From this, we can picture in our minds, a coin that represents the two sides of treatment, one being the "medication side," and the other being the "psychotherapy side."

During one particular point during the many years in which I was severely depressed, a therapist suggested that I try taking the medicinal route to better mental health. I steadfastly refused such treatment, because I wanted to *"beat it on my own."* However, having reached the point where I was so beaten down by depression that I felt unable to cope any further on my own; I took her advice and saw a psychiatrist. This was at a time when a new anti-depressant had just come out, along with a major advertising campaign that featured as its focal point, a sad and lonely blue-colored little teardrop. Then, supposedly after taking this miracle drug, the teardrop was no longer blue; nor was he sad and lonely, as now he found himself surrounded by other little teardrops. Ironically, they were still teardrops. I guess they were supposed to have been happy little teardrops.

I began a course of treatment that involved moving from one anti-depressant to another, with no positive results. One anti-depressant made my eyes dilate to such an extent that my vision became blurred. I was then put on another that caused such terrible stomach upset, that I'll trust you'd rather not know the details. Another medication, one that was supposedly tailor-made for anxiety, produced the side effect of the feeling of electrical currents running up and down my arms. With prescription after prescription, the only thing I consistently noticed was that half of the medications had not been helpful, while the other half made me feel worse than I'd felt before taking them, with side effects that made me feel physically ill, mentally confused, or nervously unsettled.

How Do I Deal With My Underlying Condition If My Doctor Won't?

As a person who has suffered extensively from both procrastination and depression, I have seen my fair share of psychiatrists, therapists, and other mental heath workers, in settings that have ranged from hospital emergency rooms to clinics and private offices. During one particularly difficult period, before I had begun to understand the connection between procrastination and depression, I visited a psychiatrist on a weekly basis for depression, as well as for the horrific anxiety, panic attacks, and heart palpitations that also plagued me.

"See if this helps and I'll see you again in one week," the doctor said as he handed me a prescription. "That should help with your anxiety, but just so you know, it won't do anything for your underlying condition." I looked at the doctor with a bit of disbelief, and replied, "Help me with my underlying condition!" Unfortunately, he offered nothing in return.

It must be mentioned that while I experienced great difficulty with these medications, it's worth noting that some persons who suffer from depression **do** benefit from them. Remember, if you are taking prescribed medications as a treatment for depression, anxiety, or for any other condition; **DO NOT STOP TAKING ANY MEDICATION UNLESS IT IS UNDER THE ADVICE OF, AND WITH THE CONSENT OF, YOUR PHYSICIAN.**

Besides the prescriptive armament of SSRIs, SNRIs, tricyclics, anxiolytics, mood stabilizers, tranquilizers, and sedatives I tried, I also explored several non-medicinal remedies such as Chamomile tea, Skullcap tea, relaxation exercises, breathing exercises, positive imagery, and yoga, but none of them seemed to improve either my motivation, or my depression. It might be helpful to point out that while anti-depressants are prescribed for depression, they are not called "anti-procrastinates," and for good reason, because they were not invented to treat procrastination.

"Payoff? What 'Payoff'?"

Many people seek the assistance of a trained therapist when they're in need of help with a difficult issue. However, can psychotherapy help a person who is suffering with habitual procrastination to overcome it?

During the initial evaluation process, one question many therapists pose to new clients is: "What do you expect to gain from coming here?" While the patient may be suffering from depression, he could be unaware that procrastination is causing his misery.

Because procrastination can be more of a "hidden problem" in contrast to many of the more typical problems that a therapist usually encounters, the therapist may not see the connection between the patient's depression and the procrastination which may be causing their depression. In addition, many therapists are trained to not make suggestions, supposedly so as not to interfere with a patient's progress. They are trained to try to bring insight to the patient, as if in understanding the cause of his distress, the patient and therapist can then work on eliminating the cause. Unfortunately, if the patient is mired in procrastination, he may not know what to suggest, and so, there is the potential that no substantial progress in the patient's fight against depression may be made.

As I mentioned in Chapter Two, it was while suffering with a terrible bout of depression that I began keeping a feelings journal, and eventually I discovered that habitual procrastination seemed to be at the heart of my poor feelings. I then tried talking with doctors and therapists, telling them that I was certain my depressive condition was coming from my habit of procrastinating, but that I didn't know how to go about acting differently. I recall one psychiatrist responded by saying, "Mr. Parker, you have *great insight*." He then added, "It's unusual to have a patient who possesses such a clear picture of his problem." To which I replied, "Doctor, if I have such a great picture of what's wrong with me, then why am I feeling so bad?" Perhaps if that professional had been trained differently, I might have improved more swiftly; however, that's an outcome that I'll never know for sure.

There are also times when, although the therapist can see his patient has a genuine problem, the therapist cannot determine its cause, and in an attempt to discover it, the patient then may be asked, "I'm wondering what your payoff is?" As mentioned earlier in this book, while most of us procrastinate because we seek temporary relief from our tasks and responsibilities, that so-called "payoff" is not what keeps us stuck in the muck of habitual procrastination. What keeps us immobilized is that we have been procrastinating for so long, that for the most part, we have forgotten how to live any other way. That said, the only "payoffs" for habitual procrastination are feelings of helplessness, hopelessness, poor self-esteem, and depression.

One reason that we habitually procrastinate today is because long ago we chose procrastination as a coping measure against stress, and then, as it became our way of reacting to that stress, it grew into a deeply ingrained habit. Like most habits, or almost anything that we do on a regular basis, the longer we "do" them, the better we get at them. We could say, "habitual procrastinators are experienced procrastinators." That's not to say that procrastination is a talent worth keeping: it isn't. However, we must admit that we've worked very hard to get where we're at, even if that's not a place we particularly like. That said, it's through the process of **willingly doing differently** that a habitual procrastinator will learn new ways, which, if practiced over a period of time, will result in new, positive lifestyle habits that will replace their old negative ones.

You can search high and low for causes to this puzzling behavior, and with the help of a psychotherapist along with a good insurance plan to help pay for it, many causes for this condition can be found: perhaps even a few practical solutions for it if you're lucky. However, unable to tolerate the side effects of the medications that I had been prescribed, and not having had great success from therapy or the other treatments I had tried, I began spiraling down into longer and deeper bouts of depression and anxiety. At times I even felt inadequate as a patient, for what I worried was another inability: that of being unable to be helped.

Which Can You Control—Your Depression or Your Procrastination?

Let's focus our attention on the word "control" for a few moments. Do you feel "in control" of your life? Most procrastinators would respond to that question with a firm "no," because they tend not to take control of their circumstances, except when they've been forced to.

Now ask yourself this: "Can you procrastinate after you've taken control of a task?" The answer to that is, while anyone can delay taking action *after* they've decided to act, if someone has truly decided to go through with an action, there's little chance they'll procrastinate, because delay would only cause an unnecessary diversion from their goal. On those occasions when you've taken control of a task, you were probably on the lookout for anything that might have had the potential to slow you down, and you probably felt in control, not only of the task, but of your own life as well.

If habitual procrastination causes low feelings in some people, then the answer may not necessarily lie in medication, but in learning how to overcome this poor habit that interferes with their lives, and makes so many people feel uncomfortable in their own skin. Just as we've taught ourselves how to avoid the tasks that provoke our anxieties, we need to learn better coping mechanisms in order to bravely face our tasks without becoming unduly upset—like human ostriches.

When You Become Willing to Control Your Procrastination—You Will Begin Taking Control of Your Depression

When asked about changing away from their negative behaviors, many habitual procrastinators have exclaimed, "But, I don't know any other way of life!" Although this may be true, still, you need to begin somewhere. When I began changing from the lifestyle of a procrastinator and into a person who takes action, I noticed that my overall depression began to fade. Instead of having to "fight depression" I saw that by working on my tasks, the sadness and gloom that always followed me, began to dissipate like dark chimney smoke that first turns gray and eventually disappears.

However, my potential to fall back into depression will always be there. I know that if I allow myself to fall back into procrastination, I *will* feel its depressive effects. That said, it bears stating that no self-help book alone can solve a person's problems or teach anything without the reading possessing the key ingredient of **willingness**. All that anyone really needs to begin changing from a habitual procrastinator is the willingness to be open to the material that follows, and to be willing to try new ways of acting and reacting to situations that may have caused you to become paralyzed in the past. You do **not** need to change overnight, nor would I even want you to try to rush through the material, because it would almost certainly lead to failure. As you'll discover in the chapters that lie ahead, patience is the enemy of procrastination.

If your floor has yesterday's underwear and socks strewn about it, your sink is stacked high with dirty dishes, or unpaid bills stare back at you from your kitchen table, it may seem to you like your situation is beyond hope, even "hopeless beyond a shadow of a doubt." However, it stands to reason that if you actually were hopeless, then you would not be reading this book, because if you truly were hopeless, there would be no point in even trying to change things. Just the fact that you are reading this book is a positive indication that you may be ready to move forward, and begin conquering the theft of time that is procrastination.

While Procrastination Leads to Depression, Taking Control Leads to Confidence

In short, the longer someone doesn't "do," the more difficult it becomes to start "do"-ing. Likewise, if procrastination continues unabated, there's a greater chance for it to become habitual, which can cause feelings of low self-esteem and depression. The habitual procrastinator feels helpless and hopeless, and is self-convinced that his life cannot possibly change. At times, decisions may be difficult, if not impossible to make, and a procrastinating person can lose confidence in his ability to handle various situations, to the point where forward movement can come to a halt.

Interestingly, there's a parallel between mental depression and another type of depression: an economic depression. You may wonder how an economic depression could be compared with a personal or psychological depression, but there are striking similarities between them. During an economic depression a business owner may feel overwhelmed by economic uncertainty, rising prices, and late payments by those who owe money. As a result, the owner may put a freeze on hiring, possibly even laying off current employees. Similar to a depressed person, a business owner may lose confidence in his or her ability to cope, and his or her world may feel a bit out of control. It's interesting to consider that on the evening of June 15, 1979, while addressing the American public, then-President Jimmy Carter said that both the economy and the people were suffering from "a crisis of confidence."

What often determines when a country has come out from an economic depression is when it regains its own sense of normalcy. Business transactions not only return to prior levels, but they hold steady over time, indicating that the persons initiating those transactions feel confident in their ability to buy and pay for goods and services. That in turn leads to a general growth in business activity and the need for more workers, who, given a better business climate and lacking the fear of not having enough money to get by on, regain their confidence and begin spending.

In the same way, a person who's been through a mental depression and has recovered may also feel that he's regained his own sense of normalcy. He feels confident in his ability to cope with the circumstances that make up his everyday world, and as a result, he feels a fresh sense of energy.

Going through a depression is akin to living in fear of forward movement, which is exactly what habitual procrastination is. Let's switch gears now and begin moving forward.

SECTION TWO

Into Action

Chapter Six

The Burden of Avoidance

S O THEN, JUST WHY DO we procrastinate? After all, does it not cause us an enormous amount of suffering and anguish? As one procrastinator said via e-mail, she felt as though she "were living in the land of bad choices," while another remarked, "The lot of a procrastinator is a second-class life."

Why Do We Fight Responsibility?

Given the misery habitual procrastination causes us, why do we continue putting off our tasks? Some procrastinators have come up with these possible causes:

➤ We're punishing ourselves because we don't believe that we are worthy of joy, success, or happiness.
➤ We were raised without discipline or the sense of responsibility.
➤ We're "waiting for mommy to do it for us."
➤ We're just plain lazy.

Whatever the cause or causes that left us with this malady, there's little good that can come from analyzing its source. In fact, when it comes to procrastination, *over-analysis often leads to paralysis.* In order to put an end to our procrastination, we need to stop asking: "Why haven't I...?" and instead, we need to start asking: "How do I change?" That is now our focus. While we will continue to analyze our behavior, we will now do so with the goal of defeating our internal opposition to productivity.

Are We Truly Aware of Our Procrastination?

To a procrastinator, there's probably nothing scarier than an unopened envelope that arrives in the mail. What's in it? Is it bad news? Is it a bill? If it is a bill, did they charge me for the correct amount? What if they made an error? If so, what will I do? The list of reasons for not opening that envelope is only limited by one's imagination. Of course, after opening it, you might discover that it was just a piece of promotional mail and then berate yourself for once again succumbing to your fears and, in the process, procrastinating. As procrastinators, while we often feel victimized by the world and all of its demands, we're actually victims of the ill-conceived coping measures that we've learned to rely on, which have turned into bad habits.

There are times when a habitual procrastinator will do almost anything in order to evade a particularly unpleasant task. Surprisingly, though, if we could stop a group of procrastinators lost in the frantic act of evading their tasks, some might deny that they had been procrastinating, and instead, would insist that they had been dealing with an unexpected and urgent priority. Of course, once that diversion is dealt with, another high-priority diversion takes its place, egged on by the nagging and nearly silent voice in our heads that tells us to continue avoiding.

So, are procrastinators ever truly aware of their procrastination? Do they ever say to themselves: "I know that I'm procrastinating right now." While most of us will occasionally admit that truth to ourselves, do we ever listen to ourselves? So complex is this behavior that many of us have perfected "the art of not doing—while pretending not to notice."

For example, I've never heard myself mentally plan out my avoidance by saying, "Tomorrow evening I'm going to procrastinate by watching television in spite of all the things I've already put off." Nevertheless, there were numerous times when I planned out the watching of five television shows back-to-back, at the expense of the personal obligations I had laying in wait; however, I never labeled that as procrastination. To me, it was just business as usual.

We Become Comfortable With Being Uncomfortable

Like many procrastinators, chaos was something I became far too used to. I wasn't comfortable with being comfortable—instead, I grew comfortable with being uncomfortable, perpetually living in a state of frustration. Here are some of the ways that procrastinators become comfortable with being uncomfortable:

➤ We constantly ask ourselves "Why do I continue to procrastinating on what I need to get done?" Yet at the very same time, we continue avoiding.
➤ Goofing off becomes second nature for us.
➤ Struggling with internal conflict becomes a way of life.
➤ Our lack of responsibility to ourselves occasionally crops up in our interactions with others.
➤ We find it difficult to relax when we have legitimate free time, because we feel guilty for all the tasks we still haven't gotten around to.
➤ We feel fatigued from the near constant states of worry, anxiety, and self-hate that plague our minds.
➤ Escape from responsibility becomes of paramount importance to us.
➤ Some of us further our escapism through the use and abuse of alcohol, recreational drugs, or other addictions.
➤ You begin to distrust your sense of judgment.
➤ We actively seek distractions just when it's time for dealing with unpleasant tasks.
➤ We find ourselves dumbfounded by the fact that our problems seem self-inflicted.
➤ We make promises to ourselves, but fail to keep them.
➤ We worry that we'll always procrastinate.

With all that chaos, why would anyone continue procrastinating? Well, for the same reasons that we do almost anything else, because by our very nature, we're habitual. Put another way, the habitual procrastinator acts in quite similar fashion to the compulsive gambler, who convinces himself that his next trip to the casino "just has to" yield a positive outcome from a scenario that actually offers overwhelmingly negative odds.

We Begin to Feel Helpless and Then We Lose Hope

As the tasks we haven't yet tackled build into a virtual mountain of obligations, we begin feeling overwhelmed, as though there will never be enough time to deal with everything; nor will we have enough energy with which to accomplish them. If this goes on long enough, we soon convince ourselves that life only seems to offer complicated and boring obligations and we then seek an escape from this mental imprisonment. As a result of this way of thinking, avoidance soon becomes an everyday norm, while productive "do"-ing becomes a distant memory from our past. We then become so accustomed to living this way, that we almost can't imagine any other way of life.

After a while, we lose nearly all confidence in our abilities. Later on, we begin to view the concept of *changing* as something else to avoid. So, even if some change were in our best interests, we'll still allow good opportunities to slip through our fingers.

We may miss out on job opportunities that offer better working conditions or higher pay because, although we may feel stuck in a rut, we've grown oddly comfortable living in it. Eventually though, sadness can envelop us if we begin to view our lives as bleak and joyless, with a future consisting only of lost opportunities and future obligations. That said, it behooves us to find purpose in our lives, and one great way of doing so is by learning new ways of dealing with our tasks, responsibilities, and obligations.

Our Distorted Outlook

When I was a habitual procrastinator, I sometimes worried that if I ever became a productive person, that might blow my cover of being an incapable adult. For example, I might say to myself, "If I were able to balance my checkbook, wouldn't that mean that I should be able to look for work and get a job?" The truth is that I was not only capable of looking for a job, but of holding one down—what's more, I was equally capable of balancing my checkbook, which I now routinely get done in only a few minutes. So, if I was that convinced of my past inability, then how is it that I am now capable of getting so much more done?

In the past, my mind filled with gross distortions that usually involved how much time and energy my tasks would take to accomplish. These distortions were comparable to large and seemingly unmovable mental boulders that I'd placed in my path. How could I get past that first boulder? It seemed impossible! And, if by some miracle, I were able to deal with and eliminate that boulder, I was sure that my path would be blocked by another boulder. Who had the time or energy to deal with them? I knew that I didn't. I was self-convinced that I was an incapable person, and like many people in this situation, I felt as if I bore the weight of the world upon my shoulders.

Willingness Is the Key

Much of my distorted outlook came from unrealistic expectations of what a task entailed, from not having a track record of successfully completed projects, and from the lack of any sort of reward system. However, before we can begin tackling any of our tasks, we need to find a good starting point; but luckily, you already have it, because it is within you.

To overcome habitual procrastination, we need to put the past behind us if we are to move forward. Our poor past experiences serve only to distort our forward-looking outlook. To restore the balance between how we think and act is as simple as developing the willingness to reduce the number of tasks that we have. Remember, you're not trying to eliminate your tasks, but to develop the willingness to simply reduce the number of tasks that await you.

Luckily, you already possess this willingness. If, right now, you are questioning your resolve, take notice of the fact that you are reading this book for a reason, and that reason is that you want a better life. That, in and of itself, is **willingness**. As long as you are willing to invoke change into your life, you have the ability to stop procrastinating. Rather than bashing and berating yourself with self-directed anger, you can choose to be open to the possibility of learning how to get things done in new and better ways.

One point that some procrastinators whom I have had the opportunity to speak with have raised, has been the question of why this book was not given the kind of title that many other self-help books have, something like: "Stop Procrastinating in Only xxx Days!" or "The Quick and Easy Way to Stop Procrastinating Forever!" The answer to that question is that I have found that learning to overcome procrastination can be a lengthy process, and that's a good reason to take a moment to remind yourself right now that patience is the enemy of procrastination.

Even if you feel hopeless or have convinced yourself that you are beyond help, keep reading, and know that your poor feelings *can* be turned around. In a sense, that down-in-the-dumps feeling could be your mind's way of letting you know that you need to find a new way of dealing with the things that have left you in the place where you now find yourself. As a suggestion, try to be empathetic to your own situation by being kind and patient with yourself.

Chapter Seven

Floating Away From Reality

IF YOU ASK SOMEONE WHO has been procrastinating for a few days what he did during that time, there's a good chance he'll reply, "I don't know. I watched some television and had a couple of telephone conversations, and then, I lost track of time." What this procrastinator has just described is what I refer to as "floating."

Most habitual procrastinators while away their time with mindless activities. Some watch television for hours at a time, others get lost in telephone conversations, or in any number of diversions. I like to refer to a habitual procrastinator's engagement in diversions as the act of "floating."

By "floating," I mean that the procrastinator isn't *grounded* or *tied down* to his responsibilities. Instead of deliberately dealing with his tasks at appropriate times, he only deals with them when he's forced to. If we spend the majority of our free time avoiding or skipping from one diversion to another, then we are "floating through life," carefree and oblivious to reality.

While floating may have a gravity-defying sound to it, it only has one similarity to weightlessness. It's like the feeling you get when standing on a high observation deck looking down at the streets below. People and cars seem to scurry about like ants in a colony. How funny it can seem, the people down below marching along and then nestling at street corners, waiting for red lights to change, while you observe, perched hundreds of yards above them. Unfortunately for us procrastinators, no matter where we are, we always seem to be on that observation deck—viewing life from a distance, and never keeping our feet on the ground.

What Are Some Ways That We Float?

There are just about as many ways that a procrastinator can float as there are tasks that need attention. Almost anything will do, just so long as it soaks up time and serves to occupy our minds. Here are just a few of the most common methods of floating:

➢ Channel Surfing:	Aimlessly flipping from one television station to another for long periods of time. Even if you can't find anything good, you simply never know just what could be on the next channel, and if nothing is found, you can always run through the channels for a second, or third time.
➢ Surfing the Internet:	Similar to channel surfing, you can breeze through several hours by taking an extra long drive on the information superhighway.
➢ Oversleeping:	As mentioned earlier in Chapter Two, "taking a snooze cruise" was a favorite method of mine to procrastinate. After oversleeping on a Saturday or a Sunday afternoon, I'd awaken to feelings of dread and self-hatred for having lost yet another opportunity to clean my place. Of course, I could have cleaned it up after awakening, with plenty of reserve energy for the job, except for the fact that I was now so bogged down by depression as I mentally wept in anguish over my apparent helplessness.
➢ Daydreaming:	Some call it "talking to yourself," while others call it "being deep in one's thoughts." Whichever you choose, it's all thought—with no action. I've lost more hours than I'd care to admit just to daydreaming alone.
➢ Addictive Behaviors:	These can range from engaging in compulsive gambling, which not only drains your financial resources but also monopolizes your time as well, to endless housecleaning, compulsive shopping, overeating, becoming overly caught up in another person's problems, and engaging in endless telephone conversations. The list of addictive behaviors that can take us away from our responsibilities is practically endless.

There are many more ways that we can float. All it takes is something that can sufficiently divert our awareness away from our tasks.

How Does Floating Make a Procrastinator Feel?

In the past, I wasn't acutely aware of when I was floating; that's how normal it had become. In fact, floating not only felt normal, it also felt comforting, putting me in a serene, almost trance-like state of "The world can wait, because this is *me* time." For example, while channel surfing for a long period of time, my mind wasn't plagued by thoughts of, "Dave, shouldn't you be doing something else?" Instead, I felt reassured, safe, and comforted. My attention was absorbed by the flickering image on the television screen and my constant channel flipping. The internal conversation that went on in my mind was, "Gee, what's on the next channel? No good! Switch. Ah, let's see. No, I don't like it. Switch again. Let's see…"

When we have a good diversion, that is to say, something that helps us to avoid our tasks, they often reinforce themselves while we're engaged in them, which then makes it even more difficult to stop engaging in them. So, the longer I channel-surfed without finding a program that I liked, the more concerned I became that if I stopped channel surfing, I might wind up missing a good program. That explains why some procrastinators find it difficult to turn their television sets off.

The act of floating covers our anxious minds in warm blankets of peace, serenity, reassurance, and safety; this helps to explain why we're so apt to divert our attention from our tasks with little regard for the consequences of our inaction—as we float away in an ignorant bliss. Although floating works against us in many ways, we might not wish to totally change from our distractions because they reward our conscious minds with feelings of security, in spite of all the upheavals they cause us.

What Happens to Us as a Result of Floating?

While my conscious mind was being flooded with those warm and reassuring feelings, I felt that all was right in my world. Occasionally, the thought of a task I didn't want to deal with would distract me for a moment, which made me feel anxious. Luckily, all I needed to do was flick my fingertip on my remote control, and a new distraction would appear on the television screen.

Given the power that floating gives us to subdue anxiety, probably faster than any pill known to man, how would you compare the act of floating to the act of say, balancing your checkbook? Which activity would you prefer to engage in?

For a habitual procrastinator like myself, floating was undeniably appealing. Because of the power it had to distract me, over time, floating changed me; it made me far less likely to sit down and deal with any task that seemed less appealing than most of my diversions. In essence, floating had the effect of conditioning my mind's willpower to wither and fade away. I can recall how, when I was a high school student, I could concentrate for long stretches of time at math and science, subjects that occupied the intellectual resources of my mind; however, due to my prolonged floating as an adult, I've lost some of those abilities. My condition reached the point where merely the thought of sitting down to some tasks became nearly impossible unless they were directly linked to dire and unacceptable consequences. For example, the only way I could sit down to balance my checkbook was if I were concerned that the bank might have made an error, and if I didn't reconcile my checkbook, I would have to forfeit the loss.

Going along hand in hand with the mental effects of floating are its physical effects. Because diversions command our attention, we are apt to lose track of time while engaged in them. We may stay up far too late watching television and then wake up late the next morning, or suffer from low energy because we haven't had a full night's sleep. As a result, we might stumble in late to work the next day, hoping no one notices our lethargy.

With All That Against Us, How Then Do We Change?

Habitual procrastinators often experience profound difficulty in seeing the good in accomplishing a task because some of its aspects may overwhelm them. They may perceive of a task as being boring or simply less interesting than a pleasant diversion might offer them. Procrastinators may also experience frustration at a task that may prove to be somewhat complicated because they haven't dealt with that sort of task in a long while. We could say their *mental muscles* were out of shape due to lack of use.

Habitual procrastinators look at their tasks as though they are standing at the foot of a mountain, craning their necks, and fixing their sight upon its crest. "How could anyone climb that? Impossible!" Thus, we tend to judge our challenges and then give up before even making an attempt at them. If we do that for long enough, we not only lose the ability to deal with our tasks, but we also lose our ability to view them objectively and to see the positive payoffs that would come from successfully dealing with them. In other words, we lose our perspective.

The typical person who is not a procrastinator deals with his tasks, first and foremost, because his tasks need to be done. His mental muscles are strong because he uses them a lot, and for different sorts of tasks. He also tends to use time, rather than allowing time to slip away unused.

In contrast, when we allow time to pass by floating, we not only get lost within one of our distractions—we also weaken our mental muscles. Given that we are so incredibly comfortable when we float, it might be helpful to begin thinking of our diversions as *insecurity blankets*. We need to begin developing the will to change our long-held ways and beliefs about our tasks, and a good way to start this process is by learning to see the good in our tasks. In that way, we can work toward regaining the perspective we thought we had altogether lost.

Chapter Eight

Developing the Willingness to Change

THE PURPOSE OF THIS CHAPTER is to lay a foundation for the concepts, ideas, and suggestions that will come later on.

Typical Sunday Afternoons and Typical Monday Mornings

During the very early days of writing this book, my then-girlfriend would visit my place on weekends. This, despite the fact that I had made a simple promise to myself, that I would take care of household chores and work on this book on weekends. However, once the weekend rolled around, I felt that Saturdays and Sundays were for relaxing, so I relaxed. Late Sunday afternoon, after she'd gone, it was too late to do little more than watch television and go to sleep. Then, when Monday morning arrived, I'd not only awaken to an unkempt apartment and an unfinished manuscript, but to a full-blown panic attack as well.

My heart raced like a team of wild horses galloping through a field, and it felt like the end of the world was upon me. Previously, I had tried to fight those panic attacks by staying in bed, steadfastly determined not to let them ruin my morning, but I could never get any sort of rest after suffering one.

Those panic attacks came each and every Monday morning, except for three-day weekends, when of course, they'd arrive on Tuesday instead! What puzzled me most about them was why they arrived only after I had had a nice and relaxing weekend. They didn't seem related to my job, because I genuinely liked the office where I worked at the time, so it had to be something else. What could it be?

The Cycle of Procrastination That Led to Panic Attacks

Those panic attacks always occurred following relaxing weekends because instead of using the time to deal with responsibilities, I instead spent the weekend relaxing. We could say, I went through a *cycle of procrastination*. Here's how the cycle ran its course:

Timeframe of the Cycle	What Happened
➢ During the workweek.	➢ I made a promise with myself to take care of household chores and to work on my book on the weekend.
➢ The weekend arrived.	➢ I focused on rest and relaxation.
➢ Sunday evening arrived.	➢ I was too tired to do much of anything.
➢ Monday morning arrived.	➢ I had a terrible panic attack.

While those panic attacks came and went with each and every weekend, sadly, I couldn't come up with a reason for them. In fact, if you'd told me that scientists had discovered that people who suffer panic attacks each and every Monday morning also suffered from overexposure to gamma radiation from outer space, I probably would have searched for a clinic where I could get tested for it. Comical as that may sound, I would have gladly looked into almost anything that may have had the power to eliminate my own responsibility for setting up that cycle of procrastination; not to mention those feelings of depression, panic, and sad misfortune that came with it.

After twenty or thirty minutes I'd slowly muster the courage to get out of bed. Feet finally on the floor, I'd get up and look around at the disorganized mess that was my apartment. Sadly, it was the same mess I had promised myself to organize and clean up the week before, as well as the week before that. Then, I remembered that promise I'd made to myself: "This weekend, clean up the apartment, and work on the book." Yet all I had done the entire weekend was to have hung out with my girlfriend, watched television, and ate. Still, I pondered, "Why do I get these panic attacks?"

There's an old saying that goes, "If you keep doing what you've been doing, you'll probably keep getting, what you've been getting." There's a great deal lot of truth in that saying. Whether or not you suffer from panic attacks, chances are pretty good that you're reading this book because you yourself are a habitual procrastinator. If that's the case, you're probably looking for a good starting point: a place from which to begin changing from a procrastinator—and into a "do"-er. That said, right now is a great time to start that change, and that change begins with **willingness.**

Developing the Willingness to Change

Today, I view those Monday morning panic attacks that I formerly suffered from in a different light. Because today, I know and understand that if I decided to place my hand above a stove's flame, I'd expect to feel intense pain. That's a pretty good reason not to put my hand above a flame, and so far, it's worked for me—and probably for you as well. As we all know, physical pain is just one of the many self-defense systems we've been equipped with by nature.

That intense pain not only prevents us from continuing a hazardous activity that we've engaged in, it also serves to protect us in the future by preventing us from engaging in it again. In much the same way, I now recognize that the sort of physical pain that I'd expect to feel after placing my hand over a flame, is eerily similar to the mental anguish that come from panic attacks and depression. In short, they're all self-defense warnings that my mind sends to alert me when I'm doing something wrong. And should I choose to engage in *any* of those activities, I'll more than likely pay a price for that decision, *or indecision*, as the case may be.

We could say that when I went against my own advice, by not taking care of the tasks I had promised myself to pay attention to, I often suffered negative consequences as a result. This is somewhat of a unique phenomena in human nature, because while non-procrastinators occasionally suffer the consequences that result from the actions they've taken and then regretted, habitual procrastinators seem mostly to suffer consequences as the result of the things that they haven't dealt with. Put another way, it's our lack of willingness to deal with our tasks, which in turn, can cause the feelings of havoc and loss of control that often leave us feeling bewildered.

I recall the day I spoke with one particular procrastinator who suffered from depression. After discovering that I was working on a self-help book, he exclaimed, "I have a bookcase that's completely filled with self-help books. I own a copy of every self-help book that's out there. I haven't really read them, but I've got all of them!" Remember: no self-help book alone can change someone's ways unless the reader is **willing** to be transformed.

Move a Muscle, Change a Thought

Your history as a procrastinator isn't as important as the direction you decide to follow. If you've fallen into the trap of habitual procrastination, there's a good likelihood that you've learned to rely on cues from your nervous system to alert you on when to take action. If that sounds like your system, then *right now* might be a good time to a discover new way of going about your tasks.

After mentioning my concerns about those Monday morning panic attacks to a friend, he told me about a saying that his mother would recite to him when he was a young child: "Move a muscle, change a thought." I gave his suggestion a try, and I found that if I forced myself to get out of bed, my panic attacks had much less of a grip on me. I'm not saying that the decision to leave bed was easy. It wasn't, especially at first. There was a big part of me that wanted to stay wrapped in those warm bed sheets. And there were a few times when I had to practically throw myself out of bed and stop myself from hopping back in it.

Sometimes, I would do a little housecleaning, just to give myself something to do, just to keep myself moving. It didn't matter what I did. Whether I dampened a sponge and dusted, or aligned the spines of some books sitting on a shelf, that saying of my friend's mother was true—the act of physically moving about helped my mind awaken out of dreamland and to greet the light of day. In short, **willingness** was what it took for me to fight back against the panic attacks that had previously disabled me.

There's a big difference between helplessly riding out a panic attack and not allowing one to hold you back, and the same is true with procrastination. While you might not like your procrastinating ways, there could be those times when you just can't seem to stop yourself from engaging in it. If there are times when you find yourself in a similar situation with procrastination as I did with panic attacks, remember that just as I successfully fought against those panic attacks, I also successfully battled against habitual procrastination. They were both defeated as a result of the willingness that I learned to develop.

While willingness helped loosen the hold that habitual procrastination had on me, there were other factors that contributed greatly to my developing it in the first place. Remember that feelings journal that I began writing while in London? Well, it was in that journal that I found some of the contributing factors for my procrastination. Let's explore some of them.

Chapter Nine

The Golden Rules of Overcoming Habitual Procrastination

IN THIS CHAPTER, YOU'LL LEARN what I call "The Golden Rules of Overcoming Habitual Procrastination." They developed out of my assessment of some of the basic areas of my life that had led me to using procrastination as a way of dealing with my tasks and responsibilities. Read through them and see how many of them apply to you.

Always Keep the Promises That You Make With Yourself

While I had wondered what kicked off those cycles that culminated in panic attacks on Monday mornings, I found that the answers were really quite simple. And, as you may recall, the word "simple" made a small but important appearance in the previous chapter when I wrote, "I had made a simple promise to myself, that I would take care of household chores and work on this book on weekends. However, once the weekend rolled around, I felt that Saturdays and Sundays were for relaxing, so I relaxed."

Many procrastinators spend a good deal of their free time looking back and asking themselves, "Why didn't I do what I needed to do, when I had the time?" This is akin to driving a car in reverse while using the rearview mirror for guidance; while it can be done, it's hardly worth the effort.

For us procrastinators, our troubles often start the moment we say to ourselves, "I need to do _____." After that sort of self-statement, we almost automatically think of a convenient, yet oddly vague time for getting around to it. Of course, when that time comes, we then do something else, or somehow convince ourselves that we've nothing else to do—in which case, we either sleep, channel surf, or help the elderly couple next door rearrange the canned goods in their pantry.

The first key to overcoming procrastination is to learn to listen to the things you tell yourself, especially when that internal message concerns a previously uncompleted task. If you make a promise to yourself to do something, I'm going to ask you to think about holding yourself accountable, because if you fail to keep the promises that you make with yourself, you'll continue to face difficulty trusting yourself to do what's needed when action is necessary. Please note that this is not an attempt to instantly transform you into a "do"-er; but rather, it's a starting-off point.

It's interesting to point out that when a non-procrastinator makes a promise with himself, he will usually deliver on it unless an extenuating reason arises and becomes a legitimate and time-pressing priority over the task that he was going to deal with. Remember that willingness alone is your biggest asset at this stage of the game, and you can make a good start at overcoming your habitual procrastination by always being willing to keep the promises that you make with yourself.

Let's now shed light on some of the other basic areas of life from where procrastination can find a toehold.

Try Not to "Compare and Despair"

While many procrastinators mention that housework is a major chore that never seems to get done, what really seems to bother them is that cleaning seemed to be a whole lot easier when they were younger. Take Ted, for instance, who says, "When I was a kid, cleaning up my room was a snap! One, two, three, done! So, why does housecleaning feel like such a horrendous ordeal today?" Ted's committing one of the prime offenses that many other procrastinators make: he's comparing his distant past to his life today.

While we all have the tendency to compare our present-day lives to our past, or other persons' lives, the results of this is often a distorted outlook, and one that can take an emotional toll on us. For example, imagine that you've just noticed people who are dressed to the nines, and they're hopping into a dreamy sports car. If you were having a difficult day, you might say to yourself, "Gee, when did I miss the boat? How come I don't have a car like that?" Does that kind of internal self-talk make you feel better about yourself, or worse?

On the other hand, if you saw a homeless person sitting by the side of building holding a worn paper cup, you might give him some spare change, but would you think to yourself, "Well, I might be having a bad day, but compared to him, I'm not doing *that* badly." Not too many of us would, because when procrastinators compare themselves to others, we only tend to do so when we're putting ourselves down.

In addition, when Ted makes comparisons to how things were when he was a boy, he embarks upon a momentary voyage to a time that no longer exists. While memories most certainly have a proper place in our minds, when Ted remembers as a response to a need (in this case, to cleaning his place), his memorializing becomes fantasizing, which is another substitute activity that procrastinators engage in to avoid their tasks. Sure, housecleaning was easier for Ted when he was a kid, but then, shouldn't it have been? After all, how does his present-day life compare to his life back then? Did he have his own place? No, he just had a bedroom in his parents' home. Did he have to vacuum or mop all the floors, including the bathroom, as he does now? No, again. Ted needs to remind himself that back when he was a boy, all he really needed to do was make his bed, neatly put away his clothes and toys, and perhaps arrange his schoolbooks for the next day. There really isn't much of an actual connection between the situations, yet Ted persists in creating one, and to his own detriment. As a grown man, Ted's life is complicated, just as much as almost any adult's life is. His chronic comparisons don't help his habitual procrastinating at all.

Another problem with Ted's habit of comparing himself to his younger-self, and to others, is it often leaves him feeling resentful. Ted's angry resentments lead him to think up self-statements within his mind like: "Life isn't fair!" While such thoughts may seem like a natural reaction, they can actually help perpetuate procrastination because it's much easier to complain about our tasks than it is to act on them.

Likewise, when we feel angry and resentful, we act a bit like the elder lion that roars at the younger lions just to show who's boss. Once the elder lion finds no one else to prove that he's "King of the Beasts," he quickly finds a shady spot and takes a nap. Similarly, after Ted has run, "It isn't fair—and it shouldn't be this way!" a few times through his conscious mind, he then does the same as the lion king; he takes a nap!

Lastly, Ted sometimes compares himself to people that, in his opinion, perform better than him. Usually, they are co-workers of his, and while Ted may be aware of his resentments of them, he may not be as aware that those resentments sometimes register on his face or in his body language.

Once again, as much as we might like to, we cannot automatically change overnight from being habitual procrastinators into "do"-ers. However, please remember that you aren't under any pressure to change. Instead, just try to be on the lookout for those times when you "compare and despair." And, should you catch yourself "comparing and despairing," be gentle with yourself by complimenting yourself for finding this mental trip hazard. Then, try thinking of another way of looking at the same situation. Then, the next time you find yourself in a similar situation, you might avoid the pitfalls that can occur when we make comparisons.

Avoid Giving Yourself Vague or Conflicting Instructions for Accomplishing Tasks

Just as some procrastinators fail to keep the promises they make with themselves towards dealing with their tasks, some procrastinators also give themselves vague and even confusing directions for how to go about accomplishing those tasks.

Ted, our friend who tends to "compare and despair," is one such procrastinator who sometimes finds himself stymied by his own logic. For instance, another reason for putting off his housecleaning is because he thinks: "There's little point in getting started if I'm not going to get it all done." This is a conflicting instruction because the truth is, Ted's put off his housecleaning for so long, that it would take a professional cleaner at least two or three visits in order to make his living space look nice.

This sort of self-statement, although very common with a lot of habitual procrastinators, is filled with the kinds of traps and pitfalls that can cause us to cease work before we've even begun. When we engage in this practice, we cause ourselves to shut down, and then nothing gets accomplished. Let's re-examine Ted's thought from the previous paragraph: "There's little point in getting started if I'm not going to get it all done." If Ted continues along this train of thought, here are just some of the roadblocks that he may encounter:

> ➤ Ted doesn't realize that his goal is unrealistic, because he simply isn't going to get everything accomplished in just one undertaking.

> ➤ When he makes up his mind to get down to cleaning, he sees only the big picture, and then he becomes overwhelmed by the enormity of it all.

> ➤ Ted concentrates on the big picture because he sees only the overall goal as the one that *counts*. He's like an army general who wants to win a war, but doesn't want to engage the enemy in small battles.

> ➤ By the same measure, if Ted completed a few tasks, he'd likely disregard the results as nil because he failed to get everything done.

> ➤ Ted expects perfection from himself, which is completely unrealistic. When he attempts to take on one of his tasks, he feels overwhelmed, and then puts it off for another day: "A day when I'm more up to it," he says to himself. Then, Ted falls into feelings of depression and inadequacy because once again, he's failed himself.

> ➤ We can observe that one reason why Ted is a habitual procrastinator is because he always concentrates on the big picture. Yet, in spite of his poor track record at housecleaning, as well as other tasks, he never alters his approach. Instead, he sticks with what he's already proven doesn't work for him.

> ➤ Like many procrastinators, Ted fails to plan. Unfortunately, Ted has yet to realize that when he fails to plan, he plans for failure.

> ➤ Ted doesn't know that if he only accomplished a few tasks in his spare time, it would be *good enough*, and that for a perfectionist like Ted, *good enough is great!*

> ➤ Like many procrastinators, Ted fails to tackle his tasks unless he's forced to by either a deadline or the threat of a penalty.

The remedy for us in situations like our friend Ted's, is to give ourselves operating instructions that are less vague—and that are more accurate. For example, let's look at how a habitual procrastinator like Ted assesses the task of gardening, followed by how a non-procrastinator views the same situation:

The Habitual Procrastinator Says	While the Non-Procrastinator Says
➤ "It's too hot to do this today; I'll get sunburned. I think I'll watch a little television and wait for the sun to go down. Then it'll be cool, and I can tackle it."	➤ "It's a hot day outside, so I'll need to do this in bits and pieces. All I really need right now is to tidy things up a little. I'll pull those daisies and that patch of crabgrass, and maybe trim the edges with a weed-whacker if it's not too hot. After that, all I have to do is water it. I can mow it tomorrow."

Notice the differences between the habitual procrastinator and the non-procrastinator. While both are faced with the same task, their differences have more to do with their *attitudes* than anything else.

The procrastinator says to himself, "It's too hot to do this today," falling right into the trap of unrealistic goals and expectations: he thinks if he can't complete it in one go, then it's not worth doing. So, he comes up with a vague, alternate plan, by thinking, "I think I'll watch a little television, and wait for the sun to go down." This is fine, except for one thing: he won't get around to it because he'll either become absorbed in watching a program, or he'll fall asleep on the couch. Either way, he'll be confronted with two scenarios that he hadn't planned on: one is that it will be too dark to mow the lawn, while the other is that mowing the lawn in the evening would probably annoy his neighbors. Whichever side the coin lands on, there's a good chance that the next day Ted will look out at the billowing sea of grass in his front yard and he'll reel in anguish, loathing, and self-dismay.

Now, notice how the non-procrastinator first assesses his situation by saying, "It's a hot day outside, so I'll need to do this in bits and pieces." Instead of having an all-or-nothing attitude, the non-procrastinator realizes that the sun has put him at a disadvantage, so he alters his plans to fit the situation he finds himself in. He then says to himself, "All I really need right now is to tidy things up a little. I'll pull those daisies and that patch of crabgrass, and maybe trim the edges with a weed-whacker if it's not too hot." By separating his tasks into manageable chunks, he decides how much he can handle and gives himself a bit of leeway, to do more or less, as conditions warrant. Finally, he gives himself permission to temporarily delay completion of the task with: "I can mow it tomorrow." However, being a non-procrastinator, he knows that if he makes a promise with himself, he must keep it.

Respond to Your Tasks in a Logical Way

Another procrastinator who finds herself sullen and frustrated is Janice, who keeps an oversized and over-stretched garbage bag containing empty plastic bottles propped between the door to her apartment and an adjacent closet. Janice keeps telling herself she needs to bring the bag down to the basement because it's grown so large that when she arrives home from work, she needs to press her full weight against the door just to open it. The bag also makes it difficult to get to that closet, which is where she keeps her commuter rail pass and pocketbook. So, she battles with the bag both after coming home from work, as well as the next morning.

"Oh, I've got to take care of this!" she says to herself before leaving for work Thursday morning, but later that evening she returns to do battle with her front door once again. "I'm going to take that bag down to the basement this weekend!" she says. "That's it!" However, come the weekend, Janice's mind is on anything but the bag, her front door, the closet, or on going to work Monday morning. So, when Monday inevitably arrives, Janice's bag of bottles is heavier than ever, and instead of dealing with the bag in a one-time effort by taking it down to the basement, she says to herself, "I don't have time to fiddle with that now; I'm late!" Later that evening, she finds herself in the same boat as the week before and bemoans the situation once more.

Habitual procrastination almost always takes its shape in the form of cycles of behavior. The cycle Janice finds herself in right now is one of responding incorrectly to the same situation over and over again, but not learning from these experiences that what has happened in the past will probably continue to happen should she continue responding in the exact same way. Instead of observing her unpleasant situation for what it is and changing, Janice floats, and then suffers the consequences of bad feelings and poor self-esteem.

The Primary Goal of Accomplishing Your Tasks Is to Increase Your Self-Esteem

When someone falls into depression, it's not surprising to hear them say they feel as though they lost whatever self-esteem they had, and the same holds true for procrastinators. Tasks that seemed practically impossible to complete due to habitual procrastination seem even less likely to be accomplished after depression has set in.

Since procrastination means not dealing with one's tasks, most especially, to the point of completion, if the sufferer has procrastinated habitually for long enough, he isn't likely to have a long list of recent accomplishments. It isn't difficult to imagine that anyone caught in that situation might then struggle with low self-esteem.

Luckily, if someone has stumbled in this sense, it doesn't mean they can't pick themselves back up. Clearly, a course of action is the action to take; however, it must be done gradually, because people who have suffered with loss of self-esteem can very easily become overwhelmed. Remember too, that small accomplishments can add up quickly into greater amounts of self-esteem. In my own case, if I have no dirty dishes in my kitchen sink, worn clothes aren't draped over my furniture, and I know my checking account balance—for a person like myself, that state is quite an accomplishment, and achieving it always bolsters my self-esteem.

It's for this reason that we must keep in mind that for us, our primary goal is not to accomplish our tasks, but to raise our self-esteem. To do that, you needn't concern yourself over *how much* or *how many* accomplishments are necessary, because all it takes is the accomplishment of just one task in order to begin feeling better about yourself.

Be Wary of Making Harsh or Inappropriate Self-Statements

If there's one question that I'd never like to hear again, it has to be, "Aren't you being a little hard on yourself?" I've heard that from more people than I'd care to remember, and it's caused me a good deal of bewilderment and frustration when I couldn't understand why other people were so concerned about me being tough on myself. After all, wasn't "being hard on myself" a sign of my determination and positive attitude? Well, they were signs, just not productive ones. And that's part of the problem that we face, because we sometimes do things that we think are productive, yet, despite our best efforts, precious little gets accomplished.

Many habitual procrastinators have a "mental radio" playing an almost constant stream of negative self-statements with which they berate themselves for not "do"-ing. Through the use of harsh or inappropriate self-statements, this negative internal dialogue not only pushes us too far, but in the wrong ways too. We do this because we fall into the trap of putting unrealistic expectations upon ourselves; and while our internal dialogues may sound sensible to ourselves while we're listening to them, they're mostly unachievable for a variety of reasons.

Our friend Ted has a similar problem with household cleaning. During the workweek he tells himself, "For once and for all, this weekend I'm going to whip my apartment into shape!" When Ted tells himself that, it only follows in his mind that it must "do"-able, otherwise, why would he think it?

Was Ted's self-statement true, or could it actually be a bit deceptive; being more complicated than he would otherwise have hoped? In addition, if his self-statement was inaccurate, could that also pose a barrier and prevent him from taking action?

Remember: our self-statements are the instructions that we give ourselves. Let's examine Ted's self-statement by breaking it down into its components to see if it provides him with good instructions.

The Components of Ted's Self-Statement: "For Once And For All, This Weekend I'm Going To Whip My Apartment Into Shape!	What Is Needed
➢ Dusting.	➢ The physical energy to move objects around, and get in close to the dusty surfaces with a cleaning cloth.
➢ Scrubbing and/or mopping floors.	➢ Ted needs to move furniture around, get hot soapy water, and then get clean rinse water.

➤ Organizing and/or filing.	➤ He needs to devote a good bit of time for deciding what goes where, and to neatly place it all into file folders.
➤ Throwing old things out.	➤ Ted will need the emotional energy with which to "let go" of items that, though unnecessary, could be of significant sentimental value.
➤ Finding new ways to use the space that had been taken up by the things he just threw out.	➤ The physical energy to move furniture and household items back where they belong.

So, how "simple" did that sound to you? This is an example where someone prevents himself from taking action because what he's told himself during the previous week while at work has little to do with the real work of getting it done.

The self-statement, "For once and for all, this weekend I'm going to whip my apartment into shape!" is what my father would have called "a pipe dream." While this self-statement cloaks itself in the guise of good intentions, it can actually prevent the procrastinator from taking action because it's more of a fantasy statement than anything else. As we all know, it's fine to dream of fantasies—they're a pleasant distraction, but we cannot live an adult life in a full-time fantasy world.

Although there are some individuals who can order themselves to whip their apartments into shape in almost warrior-like frenzy, not everyone is like this. Habitual procrastinators like us can inadvertently order ourselves to become still and frozen in our tracks, because we communicate with ourselves in the wrong way. Our mission is not to become "warriors" or to "stop acting like lazy jerks," as some procrastinators have said to themselves. Instead, our goal is simply to gain a more balanced life.

You've probably seen the manager of a major league sports team face reporters after losing a crucial game, and then praise his team for their effort by saying something like, "Well, we did our best." We can learn a great deal about positive self-talk from observing how others handle difficult situations. If, instead of putting ourselves down, we objectively examine our behaviors with the aim of finding the cause-and-effect relationships for our in-actions, we'd then realize the opportunity to see our negative behaviors in a new light. With this approach, we can begin separating our past from our future by communicating with ourselves in better ways, learning to be patient with ourselves, giving ourselves better instructions, and acting in new ways.

Understand That There Will Be Consequences for Your In-Actions

As habitual procrastinators, we generally don't like being told what to do, or when to do it—that seems to be our nature. It doesn't matter if the pressure is coming from external sources, such as bills we've put off, or our internal voice telling us that we need to clean up our place. However, it's also natural for many of us to feel depressed, anxious, and even victimized by our tasks and responsibilities. Some procrastinators feel as if they're being followed by a black cloud. If we reach the point where we rarely accomplish any of our tasks because of the multitude of things needing our attention, we may feel overwhelmed. The inevitable result of this is feeling helpless and hopeless.

However, if our backs have been pressed up against the wall by the negative consequences of an undone task, we might respond to the pressure like soldiers on patrol who've suddenly found themselves under attack. When there's absolutely no recourse, we fire back at our tasks with action: not consistent and prolonged action on one task after another, but just enough action to win that particular battle. Unfortunately for us, those battles and our chosen method of combat take their toll on us, and we then become casualties of habitual procrastination.

In a sense, we become battle-fatigued and, like experienced soldiers, we learn to practice the tactic of avoidance, which we do on an almost constant basis. Unfortunately for us, this only worsens our procrastinating ways by strengthening and reinforcing them. We fight against our tasks by ignoring them, whatever the task may be; moreover, we especially avoid those tasks that appear complicated, unpleasant, or make us feel uncomfortable. Yet despite our best efforts, "The Forces of Consequence" cold-heartedly use the extraordinary powers they have at their disposal. For example, they can shut off our electricity simply because we've been late paying our bills, and they can also stop us from taking our car out of our driveway just because our inspection sticker has expired.

If we are to begin changing our ways, we not only need the willingness to change, but also a calm and rational understanding that it is we ourselves who have placed ourselves in these battles as the result of our own procrastination. In other words, there are consequences that come from our procrastinating and, for many of us, they are the emotional ills of depression and anxiety that follow us around like that proverbial black cloud.

If we hope to overcome procrastination by accepting our tasks as part of life, we must first accept the fact that consequences follow procrastination. We also need to begin noticing that there are two types of consequences: short-term consequences and long-term consequences. Here's a comparison of them based on what happens when we put off paying our bills:

Time Span	Situation	Result
In the short-term:	Bills arrive but we shun them for several reasons: first, they're a chore. Then, you have to write out a check, enter the amount in your checkbook, and then make sure that the math is correct. Besides all that, paying bills is boring, and we'd rather do something a bit more pleasant with our free time.	So far as we're concerned, "Out of sight, is out of mind." So, we set the bills aside for some other time, and we feel a sense of relief from the drudgery of our obligations. Then, because we've essentially just told ourselves that now is time for relaxation, instead of using that time to deal with something else we've put off, we continue procrastinating.
In the long-term:	We receive late payment notices that have "Final Notice" stamped in red on the envelope. Still, we figuratively play with the bill, as if it were a toy yo-yo traveling back and forth on a string. We say things to ourselves like, "Well, they have to expect that it'll take at least a couple of days to receive the payment, so I don't really need to deal with it right now."	We feel enormously frustrated with ourselves. We wonder if we're defective, if perhaps there's something wrong with us. Mental depression often follows with its feelings of helplessness and hopelessness. Then, instead of grabbing the bull by the horns and taking back control over our lives, we start an internal dialogue repeatedly questioning why we haven't done what we should have already done, while we continue to avoid acting. Finally, when we grow tired of listening to ourselves, we seek out a therapist so we can have someone new to whom we can tell our woes.

Clearly, we need to come to grips with the fact that habitual procrastination feeds upon itself, and that when we ignore the consequences of our in-actions, we set ourselves up for untold amounts of grief in the future. In short, by running away from our problems, we cause ourselves more stress than the tasks we were avoiding ever could.

Remember That Procrastinators Are Great at Finding Excuses

We've all had as many opportunities to "do," as we've had to procrastinate. The only thing that swayed us one way or the other was the direction that we ourselves decided to pursue. What did you tell yourself at that exact moment, the moment when you could have decided to deal with that task?

In the past, I could easily come up with a list of reasons for not "do"-ing that was as long as my arm. Here are just a few of them:

➤ "It's too complicated to deal with right now."
➤ "It's boring!"
➤ "I'm too tired right now."
➤ "It's early, and I've got the whole day left to get around to this."
➤ "It's too late to deal with this."
➤ "It's been a long day, and I need to relax."
➤ "I can deal with it on the weekend."
➤ "I'm paying $75 a month for cable television and I want to get my money's worth from it!"
➤ "Maybe the reason I haven't gotten around to it up until now is because I'm not really good at this sort of task."

I remember when, back in grade school, I heard a teacher tell a student who had gotten into a fistfight, "If you look for a fight, you'll probably find one." I'd like to revise that line a bit and say, "If you look for an excuse, you'll probably find one."

Learn to Face Your Overwhelming Emotions

Whenever we encounter a task we've put off for a while, we are apt to experience either of two forms of anxiety. One type of anxiety can make us feel so panicky, it can stop us from dealing with our tasks, while the other type, which is less severe than the first type of anxiety is only felt while we're dealing with a task. That second form of anxiety produces more of a nervous, "Am I doing it right?" concern than the first form of anxiety, which can mentally paralyze us. To a habitual procrastinator, these two forms of anxiety are like a combination of swift one-two punches in a boxing ring. Ironically, although that second form of anxiety is less severe than the first type, it possesses a strong after-effect that can cause us to procrastinate on other projects.

When we initially face a task, that first type of anxiety often gives us a sense of dread and foreboding that danger is lurking just ahead. This is often based on past experiences that didn't turn out well, or when we wound up suffering embarrassment as the result of something we attempted. For example, the last time Sheila took a driving lesson, she wound up having a very minor fender bender. After that, her bemused driving instructor chuckled and said, "That's it, Sheila. You're now officially the worse student driver I've ever had!" While the comment was meant only as a lighthearted joke, Sheila was deeply embarrassed and took it as the truth. As a result, she never continued her driving lessons.

Unfortunately for Sheila, the company she works for is relocating to a place where she'll need to drive in order to get around, so she now has to face the anxiety of trying again, causing her great concern. Not wishing to lose her job, she signs up with a different driving school. Then, during her first driving lesson in years, she faces that second form of anxiety, the kind that crops up while dealing with a task, which again is less severe than the first type. While as nervous as anyone can be in that type of situation, over the next few weeks Sheila completes several hours of driving lessons and then passes her driver's license test on the first try. Yet days afterwards, Sheila finds herself procrastinating about everything. Just why is this the case?

It was the second and lesser form of anxiety that did Sheila in because, although she was overcome with fear of suffering the same embarrassment, her greater need of facing relocation in order to keep her job took precedence.

Once she began re-taking her driving lessons and then passed her driving test, she experienced a form of rebound anxiety that many habitual procrastinators feel. Sheila had her driver's license, but then said to herself: "It was so simple. Why did I get myself in such a twist over it? I'm such a stupid idiot!" It's this form of self-talk that really does habitual procrastinators in, because it leaves us looking at the rest of our put-off tasks, and makes us believe that almost anything we do will result in feelings of shame and self-ridicule.

Depending on the situation, our emotions can prevent us from acting on our tasks. Here are just a few of those anxiety-provoking situations:

➤ Fear of failure.
➤ Fear of success.
➤ Fear of mediocrity.
➤ Fear of embarrassment.
➤ Fear of being trapped in an unpleasant situation.
➤ Fear of being controlled by employers, institutions, or creditors.
➤ Feelings of frustration.
➤ Feelings of anger.

Of course, life can be complicated and demanding at times. It seems that, as habitual procrastinators, no matter how much we beg and plead with ourselves, we never seem to take action when we have the time to do so; which means that by and large, we only take action when we're forced to by some sort of crisis. Sometimes, a long history of unsuccessful attempts at dealing with our tasks combines with a desire on our part to not be bothered by obligations. When that's the case, we can become perfectionists.

Avoid Being a Perfectionist

Perfectionism is one of the most common reasons why people procrastinate. Even a non-procrastinator can occasionally act this way, such as when someone says, "If it's not good enough, I'm not even bother with it." Still, being a non-procrastinator, he or she eventually finds a valid reason for dealing with the task. However, we habitual procrastinators take things one step further by saying, "I'm worried that it won't turn out good enough, so I'm not going to try."

There's a crucial difference here, because while a non-procrastinator's attitude might be, "Let's give it a try and see what happens." a habitual procrastinator almost expects a 100% satisfaction guarantee that he will be happy with the results of his task *before* he's actually dealt with it. Put another way, while the habitual procrastinator demands a satisfactory outcome, he comes to a standstill and refuses to contribute effort or to assume responsibility for the task. If, on the other hand, he contributed effort, or in some way assumed responsibility for the task, either of those options would probably go a long way towards insuring the outcome that the habitual procrastinator so desperately seeks.

When we engage in perfectionist behavior, we say things to ourselves like:

➢ "Why can't this be easier to do?"
➢ "Just my luck. It can't all be done in one day."
➢ "I feel like it's going to take forever."
➢ "I know that I'm going to be disappointed. Why even try?"
➢ "Other people have it so much better than me."

While these statements all deal with perfectionism, they also have something else in common. If you look carefully you can see that the person making them feels pressured by time. To better see this, let's look at each original passage, and then look for its sense of timeliness:

Perfectionist Statements	What the Procrastinator is Telling Himself
➢ "Why can't this be easier to do?"	➢ "I wish it were over and done with, now!"
➢ "Just my luck. It can't all be done in one day."	➢ "Looks like I'll need to spend another day at this!"

➤ "I feel like it's going to take forever."	➤ "I can't wait until it's over!"
➤ "I know that I'm going to be disappointed. Why even try?"	➤ "And waste even more time at this?"
➤ "Other people have it better than me."	➤ "It's always going to be this way, forever!"

If we want to overcome habitual procrastination, one of the most important things we can do is to try relinquishing the overwhelming sense of urgency that causes us to feel impatient, as if there will never be enough time in the world to accomplish all the tasks we've put off. Many habitual procrastinators have a somewhat warped sense of time that makes us focus our attention on finding ways to buy time, steal time, or negotiate with time, all in an attempt to avoid our tasks. We need to become aware of this tendency, and to value our free time in order to make it work for us.

Take the Pressure Off Yourself, by Developing Patience From Within

When we try to face something that we've repeatedly put off, we're sure to feel overwhelmed by it. The longer we put that task off, the more apt we are to question our own ability to deal with it—instead of simply taking action. We may wonder:

➤ Maybe there's a good reason why I haven't gotten around to it?
➤ Could the truth be, I'm incapable of handling it?
➤ What if things go wrong?
➤ What if I wind up wasting my time?

So, with all that against us, just how do we get started on a long put-off task? The answer is: we need to begin developing patience from within ourselves, because as stated before, patience is the enemy of procrastination. By developing patience within yourself, you can train your mind to ignore side issues; in-turn, you will train your mind to calm down because it will learn to stay focused on individual objectives.

One of the best ways of developing patience is by learning to focus on doing *just one task* at a time. We'll talk more about how to do that in the next chapter.

In this chapter, we've looked at some of the more basic impediments to being a more productive person, which I call "The Golden Rules of Overcoming Habitual Procrastination. Let's quickly review them:

The Golden Rules of Overcoming Habitual Procrastination
➤ Always keep the promises that you make with yourself.
➤ Try not to "Compare and Despair."
➤ Avoid giving yourself vague or conflicting instructions for accomplishing tasks.
➤ Respond to your tasks in a logical way.
➤ The primary goal of accomplishing your tasks is to increase your self-esteem.
➤ Be wary of making harsh or inappropriate self-statements.
➤ Understand that there will be consequences for your in-actions.
➤ Remember that procrastinators are great at finding excuses.
➤ Learn to face your overwhelming emotions.
➤ Avoid being a perfectionist.
➤ Take the pressure off yourself by developing patience from within.

Now, let's move forward by learning how to deal with **just one task** at a time.

Chapter Ten

Training Yourself to Focus on Just One Task

As we discussed in Chapter Seven, habitual procrastinators tend to float away from reality by never tying themselves down to their tasks. When you don't feel connected to your tasks, it's easy to become distracted and to float away from them. In order to put an end to your habit of floating, you'll need to consider taking up a new behavior, one that's the opposite of floating, which will help you stay grounded in reality.

Luckily, there is a simple technique you can easily adopt to help overcome floating and habitual procrastination, and it can keep you focused on **"just one task"** at a time; that technique is called **"The J.O.T. Method™."** However, before we examine The J.O.T. Method™, let's take a look at an entirely different method that I once used to manage my tasks, appointments, and responsibilities—a method that yielded somewhat less than desirable results.

My Tip-Top Flop

I can recall one particular point in my life when my floating was not only out of hand, but I pretty much refused to act in any other way. I not only saw living a responsible life as something I didn't want to do, but I also actively fought against being imposed by it. One way I practiced this was by coming in late to work almost every day—not tremendously late, but just by five or ten minutes, while hoping that my supervisor didn't catch me. Of course, I was always prepared with an excuse, like saying that the trains ran poorly, or that there was a problem in my apartment and the building's super just happened to be nearby and fixed it on the spot. In a sense, my habitual lateness, just like my habitual procrastination, was my way of refusing to be tied down by a demanding world.

During that time, I noticed that many of my co-workers kept personal appointment books, and I remember feeling pleased that I was free from that sort of baggage. Imagine, having to carry around an appointment book all of the time! There were times when I would silently mock them whenever they took their appointment books out during mid-conversation, because I felt they were covertly showing off, as if they were saying, "Look how important we are, because we have appointment books!"

I liked keeping appointments and important dates in my head, in spite of the fact that this caused me to lose out on many opportunities simply because I had forgotten about them, such as a number of pop concerts that I'd missed just because of this misguided practice. Still, in spite of whatever losses I had incurred, as far as I was concerned, having an appointment book was a sign of weakness. After all, I rationalized, "If you have to write everything down, perhaps it's a sign of dementia." I then took this belief a step further by conjuring up the notion that by not writing things down, I was helping my mind stay in *tip-top* condition.

Anyway, if something were really that important, I thought, I could always write a note to myself and put it in my wallet. Unfortunately, this led to my having a wallet filled with unorganized notes, which in turn, led to ever-growing paper mountains rising atop my kitchen table. You may recall, from reading earlier, the fruitless battle I waged against those notes. I had no other way of dealing with them except for letting them lay on the table, so that in time, whatever information those notes contained had now become irrelevant and useless, which meant I could finally toss them in the trash. This way of life led me to feel depressed, as well as helpless and hopeless. At times, it even made me question my sanity.

In essence, I was breaking each and every one of "The Golden Rules of Overcoming Procrastination" that appeared in Chapter Nine. Here again are those rules in the following table's left column, along with examples in the right column of how I broke each of them:

The Golden Rules of Overcoming Procrastination	How I Broke Each of the Golden Rules
➢ Always keep the promises that you make with yourself.	➢ I promised myself that I would remember my appointments, but when the time came, I couldn't.
➢ Try not to "Compare and Despair."	➢ I compared myself with my co-workers.
➢ Avoid giving yourself vague or conflicting instructions for accomplishing tasks.	➢ I wrote reminder notes to myself, but kept them unorganized in my wallet.
➢ Respond to your tasks in a logical way.	➢ "Unfortunately, this led to my having a wallet filled with unorganized notes, which in turn, led to ever-growing paper mountains rising upon my kitchen table."
➢ The primary goal of accomplishing your tasks is to increase your self-esteem.	➢ "This way of life led me to feel depressed, as well as helpless and hopeless."
➢ Be wary of making harsh or inappropriate self-statements.	➢ Instead of focusing on my own happiness, I would silently mock my co-workers whenever they took their appointment books out during mid-conversation because I felt they were covertly showing off.
➢ Understand that there will be consequences for your inactions.	➢ I never took the consequences of this lifestyle into account, especially the effects it had upon my feelings and emotions.
➢ Remember that procrastinators are great at finding excuses.	➢ I was always prepared with an excuse, like saying that the trains ran poorly, or that there was a problem in my apartment and the building's super just happened to be nearby and fixed it on the spot."

➤ Learn to face your overwhelming emotions.	➤ Instead of facing my emotions, I rebelled. For example: "In a sense, my habitual lateness, just like my habitual procrastination, was my way of refusing to be tied down by a demanding world."
➤ Avoid being a perfectionist.	➤ "Still, in spite of whatever losses I had incurred, as far as I was concerned, having an appointment diary was a sign of weakness."
➤ Take the pressure off yourself by developing patience from within.	➤ If only I had seen my co-workers' appointment books in a more positive light, I might have had an opportunity to reflect upon how well they were organized and how they didn't seem to suffer from the low moods that came upon me. Unfortunately for me, I was not willing to change my long-held ways at that particular time, as well as for some time to come.

Obviously, if I was to overcome my condition of habitual procrastination, I needed a solid foundation upon which to build my new self.

Learning to Focus Your Attention on Just One Task with "The J.O.T. Method™"

One of the greatest ironies of habitual procrastination is that in order to concentrate on getting just one task done, we need to mentally put aside the often tremendous number of undone tasks we've yet to deal with, all of which weigh heavily upon our minds. In order to veer away from our habitually negative way of thinking, we need a good tool. For we habitual procrastinators, that tool is "The J.O.T. Method™."

The J.O.T. Method™ is incredibly effective because it's simple to use, you can easily adapt it to your needs, and most importantly, it teaches you to concentrate on the task at hand while eliminating those otherwise bothersome distractions.

All you need in order to incorporate The J.O.T. Method™ into your life are three things:

1. A pen or a pencil.
2. A legal pad or a notebook.
3. The willingness to change.

How Does The J.O.T. Method™ Work?

The J.O.T. Method™ neatly defeats habitual procrastination through an easy-to-use technique. Here's how it works:

1. Taking your pen and notebook, write today's date in the upper left-hand corner of the first page, and immediately think of one simple task that you've put off doing, and then write that task underneath the date.
2. Immediately commence action on that task and only that task. Do **not** allow yourself to indulge in any distraction.
3. After the task has been completed, lightly draw a straight line through the task, making sure that the task underneath the line can still be read.

We'll go through a few practice examples using Barry, a fictitious habitual procrastinator. If you like, you can practice using The J.O.T. Method™ by writing into your own notebook the actual day and date that you're reading this and following along with the examples.

Let's say that a few nights ago, Barry watched a DVD and after placing the disc back in its case, instead of putting the case back on the shelf where it belongs, he left it on the coffee table in his living room. This is a good first task to apply The J.O.T. Method™ to, because all Barry needs to do is to put the DVD's case back on the shelf where he keeps them so that his place will look more orderly. Let's see how Barry does this in conjunction with The J.O.T. Method™.

First, Barry writes the date in the upper left-hand corner of the first page of his notebook. Then, directly underneath the date, he writes the task that needs doing, making sure to do this **before** he takes action. Barry's notebook now looks like this:

<u>Saturday, March 3rd</u>

Put DVD away

Remember that a detailed or lengthy explanation of the task is not necessary, nor do we even want one, because the trick of The J.O.T. Method™ is keeping our instructions as clear and simple as possible. So in this particular situation, the words "Put DVD away" work just fine for Barry, because there's nothing confusing about the task or about the instruction for how to go about completing it. As stated earlier, after we've written down the task, we immediately take action on that task alone. Do **<u>not</u>** allow yourself to indulge in any distraction. In other words:

> ➤ If the telephone rings, allow the call to go to voicemail.

> ➤ If you suddenly remember that a television program you wanted to watch is on, let it go for just a few moments, because you're training yourself to focus on just one task.

> ➤ Even if the thought of something else that you've put off unexpectedly enters your conscious mind, ignore it for now, and continue with your task until its completion.

Following the instruction that he gave himself on his J.O.T. list, Barry goes over to the coffee table, takes the DVD, and places it back on the shelf where it belongs. Without pausing to do anything else, Barry goes back to his J.O.T. list and draws a light line through the task to complete it.

Barry's notebook now looks like this:

<u>Saturday, March 3rd</u>

~~Put DVD away~~

Doesn't that look neat? If by chance you hadn't noticed, the letters "J.O.T." not only stand for "just one task," they also make reference to how our method works, because when we use it, we "jot" our tasks down and then accomplish them.

Bear In Mind

When using The J.O.T. Method™, always be aware of these two important points:

1. When writing your task, use clear and simple language, because this is one situation where *less is more.*
2. Avoid the temptation to become sidetracked by distractions.

What we want to do is not only learn how to deal with just one task at a time, we also want to develop our sense of self-esteem. The J.O.T. Method™ helps in this regard because when it's used over time, it provides us with a written record of our accomplishments. It's for this reason that after we've completed our first task, we continue using that same list for the rest of that day.

A Second Example Using The J.O.T. Method™

Barry's a sentimental fellow and he often holds onto things that catch his eye in some way; but sometimes, even if he doesn't have a real need for those items, he still has a difficult time throwing them out.

Let's imagine for a moment that a bill Barry recently paid included a promotional coupon, but the coupon was only good at a store that holds no appeal to him. After paying the bill and discarding the rest of the paperwork provided with it, Barry decided to retain the coupon, if only because he wants to look it over one last time before tossing it in the trash.

Barry decides that now is as good a time as ever to look the coupon over one last time, so he writes down his new task, and his "J.O.T. list" now looks like this:

Saturday, March 3rd

~~Put DVD away~~
Look over the coupon and then put it in the trash can

It's important to point out that while the instruction needs to be written clearly, we don't need an overly lengthy instruction because that would ruin the simplicity that is so much a part of The J.O.T. Method™. So, while the instruction "Look over the coupon and then put it in the trash can" probably wouldn't be a line found in a play by William Shakespeare, it works fine for us because its message is clear, its instruction is "do"-able, and it isn't vague. Barry then follows his instruction with action: he satisfies his curiosity by looking over the coupon for one last time and then he places it in the trash can. He then completes his task by drawing a light line through the instruction, making his notebook look like this:

Saturday, March 3rd

~~Put DVD away~~

~~Look over the coupon and then put it in the trash can~~

In a certain sense, Barry has accomplished more than simply reviewing that coupon, because the reason he held onto it in the first place was because he promised to give himself a chance to look it over before tossing it away. In other words, Barry made a promise to himself to do something, and now that he has, he's honored the first Golden Rule of Overcoming Procrastination, "Always keep the promises that you make with yourself."

Lastly, as mentioned earlier, Barry sometimes finds it difficult to discard certain items because to Barry, once it goes out in the trash, it's forever gone. However, thanks to his J.O.T. list, that coupon he just put in the trash will, in a sense, always be preserved, which made Barry feel more at ease when he parted with it.

Why The J.O.T. Method™ Works

The J.O.T. Method™ not only works against your long-held negative habits, it also provides you with positive reinforcements because:

> ➤ You can now avoid distractions, because you have a logical path that you can stick to. If your attention wanders, all you need do is refer back to the last task that you wrote in your J.O.T. list.

> ➤ You're training yourself to follow self-directed instructions.

> ➤ Besides learning how to focus on just one task until its completion, you also have an opportunity to discover the positive feelings of satisfaction that accomplishments deliver and to feel your self-esteem climb.

> ➤ You not only become a productive person, but at the end of each day you have a written record of your achievements.

The J.O.T. Method™ is a simple, yet effective tool because all you need do to use it is to willingly give yourself permission to engage in the activity of your choosing. Then, after completing the task, you reward yourself by striking the task from the list. Afterwards, you not only have written evidence showing that the task was successfully completed, but with each task that you complete, your J.O.T. list reflects how productive you've been that day.

Drawing a line through a completed task has another benefit for us, because as habitual procrastinators, instead of being proud of our achievements, we often discount our efforts by second-guessing ourselves as to how much we've really gotten done. This is part of our all-or-nothing thinking. We habitual procrastinators aren't only good at finding excuses for not "do"-ing, we're also good at finding excuses for why our results weren't good enough, which is part of our tendency to be perfectionists. But now, by having a written record of our accomplishments, we can see a much more accurate picture of what we've accomplished, and feel satisfied with our efforts, achievements, and personal growth.

Lastly, the average habitual procrastinator has had a long history of suffering from task-related anxiety and as mentioned earlier in this book, they often don't feel good after having completed a task. Instead, the best some feel is a sense of relief that the task is finally over; however, that's often followed by a feeling of dread concerning what their next unpleasant task will be, and how they can avoid it. However, by making use of The J.O.T. Method™, a habitual procrastinator can develop a new sense of confidence in his or her abilities, because they only need to review their J.O.T. list to witness the undeniable proof that they're now dealing with tasks they formerly would have automatically put off.

Give The J.O.T. Method™ A Try

It's now your turn to try using The J.O.T. Method™ on some of the tasks that you haven't yet gotten around to. Do note that your starting point isn't as important as the act of *starting itself.*

Many habitual procrastinators who haven't changed their ways, live in a world of personal confusion. While they'll readily admit to having a thousand and one things to do, when asked what their first task might be, they often aren't too sure. To help speed you on your way towards successfully using The J.O.T. Method™, here's a list of some simple tasks that many procrastinators routinely put off. Feel free to pick any as your first task, to be completed in conjunction with The J.O.T. Method™:

➤ Gather up your unpaid bills and secure them with a paper clip or a rubber band.
➤ Align the spines of the books, DVDs, or CDs along one bookshelf.
➤ Give your place a quick dusting by wiping down its flat surfaces with a damp cloth.
➤ Take an empty envelope and write the word "Receipts" on it.
➤ Mop your bathroom floor.
➤ Pay one of your bills.
➤ Find an unused binder and make it your place to keep your bills.
➤ Do one load of laundry.
➤ Wash your kitchen table.
➤ Throw out the empty box that's been taking up space in your closet.
➤ Set the clock on your microwave oven.
➤ Arrange your shoes.

Try giving The J.O.T. Method™ a try right now. In the event that you're caught short without a pad of paper, several blank pages marked "Notes" can be found just inside of this book's back cover for your own use.

In the next chapter, we'll look at doing even more with The J.O.T. Method™, while still utilizing its easy-to-use format.

Chapter Eleven

Continuing Your Forward Motion

THE LAST CHAPTER INTRODUCED YOU to the basics of using The J.O.T. Method™, a simple tool that helps you to stop procrastinating by training your mind to focus on dealing with "just one task" by jotting down your tasks and immediately commencing action upon them. The J.O.T. Method™ owes its effectiveness to its lack of complexity because all that's required is your willingness to use it, along with proper use of the technique.

In this chapter, we want to continue our forward motion and begin building momentum. While The J.O.T. Method™ is easy to use, if it's not used properly, the results of inadvertent errors can wind up mimicking procrastination itself. If this occurs, a habitual procrastinator who unexpectedly meets up with renewed feelings of frustration could fall back into old ways of thinking by giving up on further action, while failing to realize that he or she unintentionally strayed from the path of simplicity. So before we kick things into higher gear, let's take a look at some of the most common road hazards that can interfere with the proper use of The J.O.T. Method™.

Improper Self-Statements and The J.O.T. Method™

As procrastinators, when the time comes to deal with a task that we've put off, we're often so used to initially looking at the entire task that we've become using to automatically searching for just the big picture. If we do that, this initial assessment can lead us to make a self-statement like "I just can't tackle it," or, "It's too complicated!" After making self-statements like either of those, our progress can come to a grinding halt.

When we reach conclusions due to the faulty instructions we've given ourselves, just as faulty instructions will prevent a computer from executing a program, our functioning can also come to a halt. Most often, this resistance to action is the result of mentally biting off more than we can chew; in other words, if we unintentionally focus on the big picture, we can lose sight of the individual steps that are required to bring a task to completion. In order to combat this misstep, we need to make certain that our initial instruction is as simple and as basic as it can be.

Perfectionism and The J.O.T. Method™

There are also times when we may inadvertently miswrite our initial instruction because of our tendency to be perfectionists. As habitual procrastinators, we often expect too much of ourselves, falsely believing that if we don't accomplish *everything* we've set out to, then anything that we have gotten done along the way *doesn't count,* meaning, it has no value whatsoever.

This belief system is counterintuitive to how The J.O.T. Method™ works, where everything that we accomplish not only counts, but counts a great deal. With The J.O.T. Method™ at our ready, we not only get our tasks accomplished, but feel better about ourselves throughout the process of "do"-ing. This is a prime reason why The J.O.T. Method™ works so well at fighting habitual procrastination, because of its ability to train us to think differently, in valuing even the smallest things we get done. However, unless you write down your initial instruction in one clear sentence, using simple and basic language, you could experience a degree of difficulty in using it.

One way to avoid being a perfectionist is to understand that it's very hard to find anything that's truly perfect. In fact, perfection is so rarely found that if we constantly seek it or expect it, then we're most certainly bound to run the risk of feeling frustrated or disappointed a good deal of the time. Given this truth, we should strive to remember that for habitual procrastinators, "Good enough is great!"

Always Be Willing to Rewrite Your Initial Instruction

If you've tried using The J.O.T. Method™ and experienced difficulty at first, that's perfectly normal—stay with it and give yourself a chance to grow into a non-procrastinator. However, should you fail to get moving on your task after a long period of time, try to take an objective look at what you've written because improper or conflicting instructions will often lead a procrastinator to seize up and to come to a standstill.

If you inadvertently focused on the big picture by jotting down an initial instruction that can't be done in a single action, you'll likely find yourself going nowhere fast. Similarly, if you've fallen into the trap of perfectionism by attaching too many conditions to your initial instruction for it to get done, you'll also find yourself at odds with forward movement. In either case, if your initial instruction seems to be vague or confusing to you, then the remedy for this is to rewrite your initial instruction.

As habitual procrastinators, we generally aren't accustomed to taking our collective will back—especially when it involves a task that we're not being forced to engage in by an external party. So for us, it's only natural that we may feel a bit flustered when we're faced with the need to rework a step, while we're in the very process of trying to get that task completed. However, it's also important to keep in mind that we habitual procrastinators are often more used to blindly going into battle against our tasks, than in keeping our eyes wide open by using the tools of proper planning and preparation. Therefore, if you find that you need to rewrite your initial instruction, although you may momentarily balk at the extra work, do bear in mind the great importance of giving yourself clearly written instructions.

How to Rewrite a Task

If a task that you've written seems too complicated to act upon, don't fret or bemoan it, just put a light wavy line through it and then re-write the same task by reconsidering what else might first be necessary in order to act upon it. Ask yourself what you need to do prior to what you had previously written down as your first step, and then write that new instruction underneath the line that you drew the wavy line over. Then, look over the new instruction and see if that motivates you to take action. Remember that The J.O.T. Method™ is not only based upon taking action on **just one task**, it also involves dealing with the smallest possible work unit that you can find in your task.

If, by chance, the new instruction you've given yourself still doesn't work for you, then put a light squiggly line through that new one as well, and give yourself permission to re-write it once again. In fact, it may take several attempts at first just to find the smallest-sized task you're comfortable with; that's fine, just remember that once you complete your task, be sure to draw a light line through the task. In addition, remember that it's important to begin building up a reserve of inner strength. One good way of doing that is by training yourself to stick with your more difficult tasks as you encounter them. Part of a habitual procrastinator's persona is to change direction immediately after he's faced adversity; if this happens to you, do your best to fight off this feeling, and continue to stay on track with the task that you've chosen to complete.

Let's pick up where our friend Barry, from Chapter Ten, left off. When we left him, Barry had just completed two tasks in the order in which he gave them to himself. After first writing down the day and date on his J.O.T. list, Barry then gave himself a simple first task: putting a DVD away in its proper place. Following The J.O.T. Method™, Barry immediately took action by finding the DVD, and putting it back on the shelf where it belonged. To complete the task, he then drew a light line through the task in his J.O.T. list. Barry then gave himself a second task, to look over a coupon that had come with a bill, before discarding it. Here's how Barry's J.O.T. list looked at the end of Chapter Ten:

Saturday, March 3rd

~~Put DVD away~~
~~Look over the coupon and then put it in the trash can~~

Now, Barry decides to pursue his third task with the aid of The J.O.T. Method™. He looks around his home and sees that his sink contains an assortment of dishes, cups, and utensils, so he returns to his notebook and writes in it, "Wash whatever is in the kitchen sink." Afterwards, his J.O.T. list looks like this:

> Saturday, March 3rd
>
> ~~Put DVD away~~
>
> ~~Look over the coupon and then put it in the trash can~~
>
> Wash whatever is in the kitchen sink

Suddenly and quite unexpectedly, Barry doesn't immediately take action upon his third task. Instead, he begins wondering if he's missing anything on television. And, unlike how he acted with his first two tasks, Barry now finds himself feeling paralyzed with anxiety, dread, and uncertainty concerning the task that he's just given himself. Even worse, Barry not only feels like the habitual procrastinator that, up until a short time ago, he always was; he worries he may have lost the *magic* he fleetingly possessed. What happened to Barry, and why did The J.O.T. Method™ fail to work for him?

Barry wasn't aware that the instruction that he had given himself actually contained two flaws. Here's how these flaws clashed with The J.O.T. Method™:

1. The instruction that Barry had given himself wasn't as simple as Barry had originally thought.
2. While Barry thought that the instruction was clear and precise, it wasn't; it was actually vague.

First, although the task that Barry had given himself seemed as simple in his mind as it did on paper, insofar as reality was concerned, washing whatever was in the kitchen sink was always a task of last resort for Barry. In fact, Barry regretted writing it the moment he put down his pen. So, although he had written down what had seemed to him at the time to be a simple task, it was only after he'd written it that he realized that the task was actually a bit deceiving. However, what Barry hadn't realized was, that unlike his first two tasks, this was the first time he had written down a task that he didn't actually want to deal with. Barry only realized this when his situation had changed from paper (his J.O.T. list) to practice (dealing with the actual task).

Secondly, while the instruction *seemed* clear and precise, its wording: "Wash whatever is in the kitchen sink," was actually vague, which caused Barry to back away from the task. Even though the message might have seemed quite clear when he wrote it, Barry needed better instructions than, "Wash whatever is in the kitchen sink" and Barry was the only person who could give himself the kind of instructions that he needed.

Back in the early days of computers, there was a saying among computer programmers: "Garbage In, Garbage Out." Meaning, that if you give a computer poor instructions, don't be surprised when it fails to execute the task you've given it. The same is true with habitual procrastinators. So, even though Barry's instruction, "Wash whatever is in the kitchen sink" seemed clear to him when he wrote it, once he put his pen down and stared back at it, it seemed to be far less a valid instruction, and much more like a vague want. While Barry still wanted the result, he felt unsure of how to go about it, and as a result, he froze; meanwhile, his mind searched for a distraction with which to fill the empty and unsettling time.

In order to understand what's holding Barry back, let's go back for a moment to the section titled "Bear In Mind" in Chapter Ten. The first line of this section's two-row table states: "When writing your task, use clear and simple language, because this is one situation where *less is more.*"

The remedy that Barry needs to accept is that the instruction he provided himself with was unintentionally faulty, and that he now needs to rewrite it in a more specific, yet less complicated form. So, even though the instruction, "Wash whatever is in the kitchen sink" appeared at first glance to be clear, Barry's lack of physical action on that task told a different story.

What Barry needs to do is to draw a light wavy line through the instruction that gave him trouble. This makes his J.O.T. list look like this:

Saturday, March 3rd

~~Put DVD away~~

~~Look over the coupon and then put it in the trash can~~

~~Wash whatever is in the kitchen sink~~

Staying with his task and not fleeing from it, Barry spent a few moments rethinking his faulty instruction. After a short while, he broke his task down further and came up with something that seemed a bit more reasonable to him: "Wash the cups in the kitchen sink." Barry then wrote his new instruction on the line directly underneath the task he overwrote with the wavy line. Barry's J.O.T. list now looks like this:

Saturday, March 3rd

~~Put DVD away~~

~~Look over the coupon and then put it in the trash can~~

~~Wash whatever is in the kitchen sink~~

Wash the cups in the kitchen sink

Having given himself a more reasonable task, Barry immediately follows through with action by washing the cups in his kitchen sink. With his new task now completed, he then draws a light straight line through the task, making his J.O.T. list look like this:

Saturday, March 3rd

~~Put DVD away~~

~~Look over the coupon and then put it in the trash can~~

~~Wash whatever is in the kitchen sink~~

~~Wash the cups in the kitchen sink~~

Afterwards, Barry uses The J.O.T. Method™ to guide him as he continues working on his original task of washing whatever is in the kitchen sink. As a result of that work, Barry's J.O.T. list grew longer, until it came to look like this:

Saturday, March 3rd

~~Put DVD away~~
~~Look over the coupon and then put it in the trash can~~
~~Wash whatever is in the kitchen sink~~
~~Wash the cups in the kitchen sink~~
~~Wash the dishes in the kitchen sink~~
~~Wash the utensils in the kitchen sink~~

As you can see, Barry needed to break his overall task down into smaller parts, and once he found the smallest unit of work, he stayed with his task until its completion. Barry now feels reconnected with The J.O.T. Method™, and his notebook proudly displays his achievements for this day. Barry can continue using his notebook the next day as well, which will provide him with an added incentive—he'll see his productivity from the day before while working on whatever tasks he chooses to do on Sunday.

Do More While Writing Less

After you've used The J.O.T. Method™ a few times and gotten comfortable with it, you'll soon find that you don't need to spend as much time thinking out your tasks as you did in the beginning. This is because you'll instinctively begin searching for the smallest units of work so you can write it down, get it done, and draw a line through it on your J.O.T. list. In fact, you may find that the last part of process, drawing a line through each completed task, to be mildly addictive, spurring you on to get even more accomplished.

One surefire way to speed up your productivity is to incorporate a few simple abbreviations into the process of using The J.O.T. Method™. Here are a few abbreviated entries that will soon appear in Barry's J.O.T. list:

Abbreviation	What It Expresses	How They Appeared in Barry's J.O.T. List
"C/B"	I need to call back _____.	C/B Fred Smith
"G/T"	Go through _____.	G/T old magazine
"L/M"	I left a message on Janet Sawyer's voicemail.	Call Janet Sawyer – L/M
"L/U"	Look up or get information on _____.	L/U budget hotels located in San Diego
"P/A"	Put the _____ away so that it's not cluttering up the kitchen table.	P/A George's business card
"T/O"	Throw out the bag of old newspapers.	T/O bag of old newspapers

Let's now add those examples to Barry's J.O.T. list as his entries for Sunday, and see how it looks:

Saturday, March 3rd

~~Put DVD away~~
~~Look over the coupon and then put it in the trash can~~
~~Wash whatever is in the kitchen sink~~
~~Wash the cups in the kitchen sink~~
~~Wash the dishes in the kitchen sink~~
~~Wash the utensils in the kitchen sink~~

Sunday, March 4th

C/B Fred Smith
~~G/T old magazine~~
~~Call Janet Sawyer — L/M~~
~~L/U budget hotels located in San Diego~~
~~P/A George's business card~~
T/O bag of old newspapers

You probably noticed that the first and last entries in Barry's J.O.T. list did not have a line drawn through them. You may also be wondering why Barry's violated the third rule of working with The J.O.T. Method™ which stated: "After the task has been completed, lightly draw a straight line through the task, making sure that the task underneath the line can still be read.

Although one of the basic rules of The J.O.T. Method™ is not moving beyond a task unless it has been accomplished, there will be occasions when although you've tried your very best, circumstances just won't be in your favor and you will not be able to complete the task at the time you've chosen. That's just how life goes sometimes. However, it's good to know that by already having a task written down in your J.O.T. list, this makes it much easier to come back to. In addition, when a task doesn't have a line struck through it, that task clearly stands out from the pack.

What can Barry now make of his J.O.T. list? Well, he's had a couple of productive days and it looks like he's gotten back on track: not too shabby for a habitual procrastinator like Barry, huh? Barry knows that he still needs to call back Fred Smith, even though he already tried to do so. How do we know that he already tried to call Fred? Because, according to the rules of The J.O.T. Method™, after writing down a task we then take immediate action upon that task, with no diversions of any kind. If we accept The J.O.T. Method™ as a tool that will work for us, and if we decide to use it as it was intended, then we need to do just that: use it as it's meant to be used.

When Barry rang Fred, he didn't get voicemail; he got a busy signal instead. That's why Barry still needs to call Fred; however, just because Fred was unreachable, that doesn't mean Barry should stop everything and keep redialing Fred exclusively. Now that the incomplete telephone call had already been written down on his J.O.T. list, Barry was free to choose his next task, so he went through an old magazine that he just wanted to skim through. Then he called his friend Janet Sawyer, but he only got her voicemail, so he left her a message. Barry then went on the Internet and looked up budget hotels in San Diego for his upcoming vacation, and after that, he found the business card of his friend George, and put it away in a good place he'd remember so it wouldn't continue gathering dust on his coffee table. Needless to say, Barry doesn't draw a line before completion of what seems like an easy task, nor does he wait until he has a bunch of tasks completed to draw lines through them. Instead, as each of these tasks is completed, he draws a light line through the corresponding item on his J.O.T. list.

A Place for Everything, and Everything In Its Place

The quote, "A place for everything, and everything in its place" has been attributed to everyone from Isabella Mary Beeton to Benjamin Franklin. Being a very old quote and sounding like something that your grandmother might have told you, it's easy to dismiss what for we procrastinators is actually quite good advice.

In order to get the most out of The J.O.T. Method™, and change from being a habitual procrastinator into a "do"-er, it's best not to keep reinventing the wheel when it comes to certain tasks that we'll tend to repeatedly deal with such as the organizing of *little things*. Let's say that like many other procrastinators, you've become accustomed to allowing certain areas of your home to become unofficial gathering places for things of one sort or another. This can include anything from your collection of antique cufflinks, to your income tax statements for the last fifteen years.

I've noticed that habitual procrastinators on the whole tend to be a bit less organized than non-procrastinators. One reason for this can be found in yet another old saying: "Out of sight, is out of mind." To most people this means: "If you do not see something for a period of time, you may stop thinking about it." However, to procrastinators it can have an entirely different meaning, that of: "If I can't see it, I might not be able to find it when I need it!" This is especially apt when it comes to bills, the checkbook, receipts, and items that relate to taxes and/or bookkeeping. It's for this reason that it's important to have a dedicated place set aside for the things we want to hold on to; such as in this case—business cards, and a good starting point might be to place that card in the corner of a desk drawer. That way, he can keep all the business cards that he already has, as well as those he brings home in the future, together in one place.

Barry now completes the last task on his J.O.T. list by removing the bag of old newspapers that he keeps under his kitchen sink, which is probably as good a place for storing them as anywhere in his home, and takes it out to his recycling bin. However, what if Barry was still unable to connect with Fred Smith? What should Barry write in his J.O.T. list to make sense of it all?

What Do You Do If You Have Uncompleted Tasks on Your J.O.T. List?

Once you get the knack of using The J.O.T. Method™, you'll soon discover that many of the tasks that you would have considered un-"do"-able in the past, are now, more or less, routine. Soon, you begin developing confidence in your abilities, and the little tasks that once immobilized you now seem a lot less threatening. You might even begin to think nothing of filling your notebook with lots and lots of them. In other words, the more that you do, the more capable you become.

If you could perfect the use of The J.O.T. Method™, then you would only write one task at a time, "do" that one task, and then draw a line through that task. However, we can't get everything done in a day, as much as we wish we could. This was the case with the telephone call that Barry tried to make to Fred Smith. What Barry now needs is a logical way to transfer his undone tasks from the end of his current day to the next day. He needs his transfer method to be clear and simple in format so that his J.O.T. list readily conveys his task's new status, indicating that it is undone from the day before.

In order to properly transfer his task of contacting Fred Smith by telephone from his Sunday J.O.T. list, Barry places this task in brackets, making it appear as "[C/B Fred Smith]". Barry then copies this unaccomplished task from Sunday, as his first task for Monday. Here's what Barry's J.O.T. list looked like on Monday:

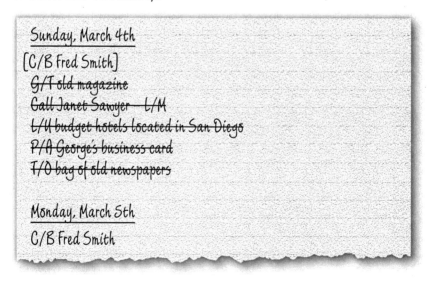

Sunday, March 4th
[C/B Fred Smith]
~~G/T old magazine~~
~~Call Janet Sawyer   L/M~~
~~L/H budget hotels located in San Diego~~
~~P/A George's business card~~
~~T/O bag of old newspapers~~

Monday, March 5th
C/B Fred Smith

Barry then tried to contact Fred Smith by telephone, but still could not reach him, so while Barry waited for Fred to return home, he filled in the time by finding a few small tasks to take care of. This made Barry's J.O.T. list appear like this:

Sunday, March 4th

[C/B Fred Smith]

~~G/T old magazine~~

~~Call Janet Sawyer – L/M~~

~~L/U budget hotels located in San Diego~~

~~P/A George's business card~~

~~T/O bag of old newspapers~~

Monday, March 5th

C/B Fred Smith

~~Mop living room floor~~

~~Plug new keyboard into computer~~

~~T/O old newspaper~~

~~P/A business card~~

~~T/O old newspaper~~

~~Change shoelaces on black shoes~~

T/O old newspaper

As it turned out, Barry finally reached Fred on Monday, after Barry had thrown out his third old newspaper that evening. And as you can see in the next and last diagram concerning what you should do when you have uncompleted tasks on your J.O.T. list, Barry drew a line through both his first entry for Monday, as well as his last entry for that day:

Sunday, March 4th

[C/B Fred Smith]

~~G/T old magazine~~

~~Call Janet Sawyer — L/M~~

~~L/U budget hotels located in San Diego~~

~~P/A George's business card~~

~~T/O bag of old newspapers~~

Monday, March 5th

~~G/B Fred Smith~~

~~Mop living room floor~~

~~Plug new keyboard into computer~~

~~T/O old newspaper~~

~~P/A business card~~

~~T/O old newspaper~~

~~Change shoelaces on black shoes~~

~~T/O old newspaper~~

So, if you run across a situation where you weren't able to accomplish a task that you wrote down, it doesn't mean that you're a failure or that The J.O.T. Method™ has failed you. Simply bracket the original item—and then copy it to the following day's entry on your J.O.T. list. Then, the next day, you'll already have a simple task to accomplish, which will add a bit of extra meaning to your day.

In addition, we've all encountered the problem of saying to ourselves that tomorrow we need to take care of a particular task, but then when tomorrow arrives, for one reason for another, that task slips our minds. However, The J.O.T. Method™ provides us with an additional side benefit: we can begin writing our next day's tasks today. Plus, if today we write down a task that's meant for tomorrow, it's helpful just to have tomorrow's task lightly drummed into our conscious minds while working on today's tasks, especially if that task is something important, like keeping an appointment.

Getting Even More Out Of The J.O.T. Method™

Always keep in mind that your J.O.T. list will provide you with reassurance that the work that you've been doing *counts*. After all, if you've taken the time and trouble to write a task down, and then came back to it on paper to put a completion line through it after its accomplishment, it must be valuable!

Here's a cavalcade of reasons why The J.O.T. Method™ will continue helping you:

➢ The J.O.T. Method™ helps slow down your thinking so you can decide what you want to do, and then do it. This makes you feel more in control of your life.
➢ You now know that your tasks don't need to overwhelm you, because you can provide yourself with step-by-step instructions.
➢ Handling your tasks one-by-one in order calms you, by lowering your level of anxiety concerning the rest of your tasks because you now have the ability to concentrate on dealing with just one task at a time.
➢ When you are almost constantly doing small things, there's almost no time to be depressed.
➢ Instead of worrying over everything you haven't done, you can focus your attention on your list of accomplishments.
➢ You gain confidence in the decisions that you've made.
➢ You restore confidence in your decision-making ability.
➢ You restore balance in your life.
➢ If you feel low, like you haven't accomplished anything because you've felt incapable, you can look at your J.O.T. list, see some accomplishments, and say to yourself, "Well, I got a few things done!"
➢ Eventually, you begin to see that you've been developing self-discipline from all this "do"-ing.
➢ Over time, you notice that you are routinely able to do more than you ever could.
➢ "Do"-ing used to be "bor"-ing, but doing it "just one task" at a time, The J.O.T. Method™ way, makes it an interesting challenge!
➢ You learn that when you write a task down, that makes it seem more important than almost anything else. You then use that knowledge to your advantage by continuing to write your tasks down, which motivates you to "do" even more.

Keep With It!

Remember that The J.O.T. Method™ is also a tool that will help you develop your overall level of patience, and as stated many, many times before, patience is the enemy of procrastination.

Keep using the same notebook because in time your J.O.T. list will become a record of your accomplishments. It will prove to you time and time again that you persevered and followed through with your tasks until their completion. As your list of accomplishments grows, your list of undone tasks will become shorter—and as that burden recedes, it shouldn't be surprising that you'll probably feel a lot better about yourself.

If you experience any difficulty with The J.O.T. Method™ at this point, try not to become too concerned. Keep tasks simple for now and get used to "do"-ing. The present time may not yet be the right time to reconcile your last six months' worth of bank statements; however, you can always work on building up to that. The most important thing to "do" right now is to become accustomed to doing in this new way.

Chapter Twelve

Dealing with Setbacks

No one sets out to become a habitual procrastinator—instead, we develop procrastination as a method of coping with life's obligations. It might not be the best way of dealing with things, but for better or worse, it allows us to continue functioning. In a sense, habitual procrastination is akin to alcoholism because while no one ever sets out to become a problem drinker or to develop a drinking habit, it happens because no matter the downfall, drinking offers some degree of comfort, relief, and escape from life's obligations. Despite all the misery that such a lifestyle begets, the alcoholic grasps his lifestyle in the same manner with which he clings to his bottle, because no matter the consequences—comfort, relief, and escape are all that he believes he needs.

Problem drinkers sometimes find their way into treatment for one reason or another. It might have been a court-ordered mandate, or they could just find that a folding chair at an Alcoholics Anonymous meeting offers more support than a tavern's barstool. However, not every problem drinker gets it on his first time around. Sadly, sometimes the saying, "Better the devil you know, than the devil you don't" holds true. Why is this the case?

One reason is because we're human, and in spite of whatever might be best for us, or our best intentions, we can slip back into familiar ways that while negative, may hold us in their spell of attraction. Just as no social drinker ever sets out to become an alcoholic, no one who puts off a task ever intends to become a habitual procrastinator. Unfortunately, it happens all the same. So what are we frail humans to do? Sometimes, the only thing you can do is to lick your wounds, and then re-commit to working on yourself.

Changing away from a long-held habit like procrastination isn't as easy as changing from one pair of shoes to another. Change happens as part of a process, and while The J.O.T. Method™ will work if it's applied in your life, it cannot work if you fail to practice it. While there may be days when you fall back into old ways, should you string a few of those days together, you may soon feel as if the method is no longer working. Changing from life as a habitual procrastinator—into a "do"-er takes time, practice, and, above all else, the willingness to stick with the process.

What follows are some of the most common situations that cause habitual procrastinators to stumble on the road to recovery. We'll also discuss suggestions for overcoming these trip hazards.

Unrealistic Expectations

As recovering procrastinators, one of our greatest potential setbacks is our penchant for expecting more from ourselves than is reasonable for particular situations. We suffer from this problem because our past habit of procrastination has shaped the ways in which we perceive our tasks. Even if we eliminate procrastination to the best of our abilities, our old ways can still occasionally crop up in our thoughts, especially when a task seems complicated or boring.

Here are some examples of our self-talk when we react to our tasks with unrealistic expectations:

➢ "It's going to take forever to get done!"
➢ "I cleaned all morning, but there's still more to do."
➢ "I've got too much to get done, it's no use!"
➢ "Only I could get so behind on things."

We always need to remember to focus on what's in front of us, rather than looking at the big picture, which is how we looked at our tasks in the past. On the occasions when we find that we've slipped back into our old ways of thinking, we need to stop, and take a moment to think up an internal rebuttal to the thoughts that pollute our minds and stop us from taking action. Here are those same thoughts from the above examples, along with positive rebuttals to those thoughts:

Unrealistic Expectations	Positive Self-Rebuttals
➤ "It's going to take forever to get done!"	➤ "I'm looking at the big picture, and I need to refocus my attention on handling just one task at a time."
➤ "I cleaned all morning, but there's still more to do."	➤ "Look at how much I've gotten done. Not everything has to be done in one day."
➤ "I've got too much to get done, it's no use!"	➤ "I need to stop looking at the big picture, and deal with my tasks on a one by one basis. It would be helpful if I wrote down what I get done, so I can see my progress."
➤ "Only I could get so behind on things."	➤ "I'm only human. I need to be a bit more gentle with myself."

The above examples serve to point out why it's important to write down your achievements, which is what takes place when you use The J.O.T. Method™. When you write down each task before it's begun and then put a line through that task after it has been taken care of, you not only wind up with completed tasks, but your J.O.T. list also provides you with a written list of your achievements. This not only shows you what you've done, it also trains your mind to see your unaccomplished tasks as the smaller components of your larger needs. No matter how large a task may be, it can always be broken down into smaller parts, and no matter how small a task may be, if it's dealt with, it's an accomplishment!

Reconsider What a "Reasonable Goal" is to You

Related to the problem of having unrealistic expectations, many recovering procrastinators put themselves under unnecessary pressure due to the unreasonable goals they put on themselves. This behavior is like that of a person who's recently given up smoking, but still leaves home with his cigarette lighter in his pocket. If that person is going to live life as a non-smoker, it's probably best that he chuck the lighter in the trash in order to avoid playing games with temptation. In the same way, if you are going to live your life as a newly minted non-procrastinator, then in order to experience the growth that you desire, then you're going to have to accept a few challenges until you become acclimated to them.

If you spot a task that needs doing, but instead of taking action, you find yourself getting lost in unimportant distractions, try listening in on your internal dialogue. Do you ever tell yourself anything like, "This Saturday, I'm going to clean out the garage," or "I'd like to lose ten pounds, so I've got to exercise like crazy." Yet then you wind up sitting on the living room couch with a tub of ice cream in one hand and the television's remote control unit in the other. If so, you may be giving yourself unreasonable goals.

Remember, one of the chief reasons that procrastinators put off tasks is because we often give ourselves vague or conflicting instructions for accomplishing our tasks. If that's the case, then we need to work on our goals, and the best way to do this is by putting them down on paper. On paper, our thoughts are less fleeting and scattered, and we have an opportunity to rework them to give ourselves a better chance of accomplishing what we really want to get done.

Here are those two unreasonable goals from above once more, but now they've been reworked as realistic goals, as you'll see in the right-hand column:

Unreasonable Goal	Realistic Goal
➤ "This Saturday, I'm going to clean out the garage."	➤ "If I can clear up four square feet of space in the garage over this weekend and the next one, that would be great!"
➤ "I'd like to lose ten pounds, so I've got to exercise like crazy."	➤ "If I want to lose ten pounds, then I'm going to have to dedicate myself to that goal by watching what I eat and getting thirty minutes of exercise, three times a week."

Your internal dialogue sets your goals, and it has the power to tell you what not to do, or what to do, so listen carefully to the things you tell yourself, and decide whether you've been flying on auto-pilot. If you don't like the direction you're headed in, then retake the controls and chart a new direction by deciding to take on the things that you can manage. It's good to challenge yourself every now and then, especially when it comes to the way in which you approach your tasks. This will often require you to break your larger tasks down into smaller pieces. Like the old saying goes, "How do you eat an elephant?" The answer is simple: "One bite at a time."

What To Do When Frustration Gets the Better of You

If there's anything that can stop a habitual procrastinator in his tracks, it's the feeling of frustration. In fact, there's nothing else that puts the brakes on action quite like frustration. Frustration is a potent adversary, but luckily, there are some things that we can do to neutralize its unwanted effects. Here are a few of them:

Frustration Fighters	How They Help
➢ Exercise.	➢ There's nothing that can get you moving, like moving will. I can't tell you how many times I got up from my computer keyboard while working on this book, if only to stand up and move my legs up and down. It didn't burn too many calories, but it got my blood moving, most especially, to my head. As stated earlier in Chapter Eight: "Move a muscle, change a thought."
➢ Lower your expectations.	➢ You're human, and like it or not, you can only do so much in one day; so try not to overwhelm yourself with unreasonable expectations. Be happy with what you can honestly get done, and take note of those things that you can't, because you can always do them tomorrow. In this situation, getting to them tomorrow isn't procrastination; it's being realistic.

➢ Reassess your goals.	➢ Have you set a goal for yourself that may not be possible at the moment? There are times when recovering habitual procrastinators will raise the bar too high, because now that they've begun getting things done, they feel invincible. Don't allow yourself to fall into that trap. Write your goals down, execute them using The J.O.T. Method™, and remember there are times when we need to crawl before we can learn how to walk.
➢ Try working at your task in silence.	➢ One of the most common problems habitual procrastinators face is the need to deal with tasks that are complicated, boring, or seem to drag on. To fight the boredom that sometimes accompanies such tasks, procrastinators will often employ playing the radio, music, or even the television in order to liven things up or to feel less alone. Unfortunately, such tactics usually backfire on us for a plethora of reasons. We'll discover more about that in our next segment.
➢ Increase your capacity for patience.	➢ Always practice patience, not just because patience is the enemy of procrastination, but because you will increase your tolerance for the world as it is, as well as for your own frailties. The less that we fight reality, the more we accept it. One of the best methods that I've found to increase patience within myself has been to slowly chant "Patience" to myself a few times in a low voice, as if it were a mantra. "Pa-ti-ence, pa-ti-ence, pa-ti-ence" slowly and calmly. Try it yourself and see how it provides you with a few moments that you can use to refocus your mind back onto your task.

When it comes to fighting the feeling of frustration, what's truly important is to find what works for you. Think back to a time in your life when you felt the same way, but persevered. It may have been when you were in school and had to study for an important exam. Or, perhaps as an adult you needed to acquire a professional license in order to qualify for an employment opportunity that you wanted. Remember what you did in order to stay focused on the task at hand. For example, while writing this book, I was faced with dealing with the noise that came from living in an apartment building. I then recalled that I had a pair of noise-canceling headphones in my closet that were just gathering dust, so I put them to use. It seemed a bit odd at the time, to be wearing headphones and to not have them plugged into anything, but I needed silence in order to do my best work. Today, those headphones are always at the ready to help when I need to concentrate while working in noisy conditions.

While noisy conditions from the outside world are one thing, there's another source of noise that stops many people from taking action; however, it's one where they have all the control, provided they're willing to reclaim it.

All I Get From My Television is "Interference"

If there's anything that interferes with getting tasks accomplished, it has to be squandering of hours by aimlessly watching television.

Many habitual procrastinators find that their television set is an enormous barrier to productivity, and for good reason; yet they always seem to have good reasons for keeping their television on. Here are just a few of them:

➤ "Television covers up my loneliness. My home is lonely if I don't have the television or radio playing."
➤ "Watching television keeps me distracted from all the things that I don't want to think about."
➤ "Television immobilizes me. It hogs my attention more than radio ever could because television almost requires that you watch it."
➤ "Sometimes, after I've been out for an evening, there's a part of me that wonders if I missed anything on television."
➤ "Television—seriously, my life revolves around it."
➤ "Television acts as my security blanket."
➤ "The time I spend watching television could better be spent doing other things."
➤ "Sometimes during the week, I record more than I can realistically watch, and then new programs air over the weekend that I want to watch."
➤ "On weekends, I escape by watching television."

> ➢ "I know I was supposed to get around to my chores, but there were so many television programs that I might have missed."

Almost ironically, the advent of the DVD hasn't helped us because, instead of using them to watch what we want, and when we want to, we often continue aimlessly channel-surfing. No matter whether we watch DVDs or regular TV, once we turn our televisions on, there's often little chance that we'll turn them off until just before bedtime.

By engaging in aimless channel surfing, we are involving ourselves in a behavior that we've explored before: floating. Planning free time is very difficult for procrastinators; in fact, it's one of our toughest challenges. This brings us back to one of our older questions, "Why am I a 'do'-er at work, but not at home?" The answer is because we have not planned out our free time at home.

In short, watching television aimlessly for hours at a time is like consuming candy bars in place of a proper meal—you'll find yourself temporarily feeling filled and satisfied, but you'll feel sick and empty a few hours later. Television temporarily satisfies you by making you feel as if you've been productive; after all, you really have done something—you watched television for several hours. However, there's no real payoff because nothing in your living environment winds up getting taken care of.

Many of our tasks require concentration if we are to accomplish them. Television not only diverts our attention from our more complicated tasks, but it also soothes us by temporarily allaying our fears over our unproductive ways by diverting our attention away from our real needs. In a sense, our television sets are like adult pacifiers. Just as prescription sedatives can calm our nerves but carry the potential drawback of addiction, television can also soothe our nervous systems, but it too can lead us down its own path of addiction. When our televisions are on, it's difficult to shut them off because that might leave us facing our undone tasks. So, the best thing to do is to leave your television off for a set amount of time, especially when you arrive home from work, and have a plan (such as your J.O.T. list with one or two tasks to take care of) and then plan out your television viewing.

If you believe that you've lost control of your television viewing, here are some suggestions that may prove helpful:

➢ Try not turning your television on the moment you arrive home. See if you can go thirty minutes without it, and use that time to complete a few items from your J.O.T. list.
➢ Allow yourself to experience the feeling of willingly going without television without first looking at the program listings. To the best of my knowledge, no one ever died or became ill from leaving their television off.
➢ Think of all the things that you could engage in if you gave up television for one night.
➢ Have your J.O.T. list at the ready so you can refer to it to see what tasks you've written down that need "do"-ing.
➢ Become accustomed to working in silence and see how much more you get accomplished.

Getting along without television isn't easy, but that doesn't mean you can never watch it again; it just means that you need to learn to be a bit more precious with your free time. Take me for example—while conquering television's former hold on my life, I wrote down a few observations in my feelings journal. Here are a few of them:

➢ "How did I get so much done last night? No TV—none. Without the television on, time slows down."
➢ "Doing without television is making peace with myself."
➢ "After I worked at my tasks yesterday morning, I thought that the reason I had gotten things done might have been because I worked in the morning, but it wasn't. It was because the television wasn't on."
➢ "Now that Sunday night is over, am I bothered that I missed television? No. Why? I'm not concerned with what I'm not aware of. You can't miss what you never had."
➢ "Two nights without any television whatsoever. It's amazing what you can get done without the television set vying for your attention."

One neat solution to aimless channel surfing that may work for you is to cut off your cable or satellite provider and go back to receiving your channels the old fashioned way, off the air. With fewer channels at your beck and call, you may find channel surfing less tempting. Some cable and satellite providers offer their customers the opportunity to temporarily disconnect their service by going on "vacation" status. This is an excellent way to experiment with living without so many television channels.

Wipeout!—Surfing the Internet

Similar to the way television can lure you into aimless channel surfing, the Internet has the same ability to gobble up the free time that we can often better employ by being productive. In fact, the two are so similar in nature, that I could practically reproduce the previous section right here, merely substituting the word "Internet," where "Television" would have appeared.

Instead of doing that, I'll simply suggest that if surfing the Internet has been monopolizing your free time, then you may wish to begin monitoring how you spend that time. If your time on the Internet has gotten out of hand, then ask yourself the following:

> ➢ Do you turn on your computer the moment you come home from work and then immediately plunge into checking your e-mail?

> ➢ Do you spend more time communicating with friends online than you do self-communicating by assessing your own needs and seeing that they're taken care of first?

> ➢ Do you get lost in Internet chat rooms, or on social networking sites?

Once again, as with aimless television channel surfing, the habit of aimlessly surfing the Internet comes down to the decisions that we make about how we will spend our free time. While it can be tremendously difficult to pull yourself away from your computer, the best way to deal with this foe to personal productivity is to avoid getting onto the Internet without first having taken care of a few pressing tasks. Once you've taken care of your responsibilities, there's no reason why you shouldn't enjoy yourself.

Alcohol and Recreational Drugs

While my understanding of habitual procrastination, its causes, and some of its cures runs deep within my life, I would be out of my scope if I attempted to give advice to readers whom I did not know, on how to deal with alcohol or substance abuse. However, there are some facts that most of us can agree on.

First, the misuse of alcohol or recreational drugs can lead to a person losing his or her motivation: this is especially true when it comes to the use of marijuana. When a person uses drugs in order to surround him or herself in the warm glow of inebriation, he or she usually feels free of responsibility and persons who regularly drink or do drugs run the risk of being lulled into a false sense of security. If the person partakes in this activity on a regular basis, he or she may lose sight of the importance of keeping on top of his or her tasks.

This can lead to habitual procrastination caused by substance abuse, with the sufferer falling into a cycle of procrastination fed by the alcohol or drugs involved, but presenting the same problems as habitual procrastination—feelings of depression, hopelessness, and helplessness. If you are struggling with the abuse of alcohol, or if your use of drugs has turned from a recreational activity to a daily one, then seek help. Find a professional treatment center, or contact your local chapter of Alcoholics Anonymous or Narcotics Anonymous. Their telephone numbers should be listed in your local White Pages directory.

Since an ounce of prevention is worth a pound of cure, here's a short summary of preventative measures to help you avoid stumbling on the road to productivity:

Work at Developing Your Positive Self-Talk:

> ➤ **Do you find that you talk nicer to the people around you, than you talk to yourself?**
>
> Since many habitual procrastinators routinely put themselves down, if you want to stop procrastinating, you may not only need to start acting in new ways but you may also need to stop thinking in old ways. Give yourself a break and treat yourself with the kindness that you deserve.

> ➤ **Learn to reframe your tasks and difficult situations.**
>
> Have you ever seen an old painting that was then set in a different frame? If so, you likely saw details in the picture that you had not previously noticed. However, the painting didn't change—only the frame did. In the same way, how we look at something is just as important as what we choose to look at. If a task seems horrendous, try to reframe it. For example: If a tax payment deadline has you down, think of how you'd like your tax money spent, and consider that by getting your return filed, you're helping that part of the system that you like to make this a better place. Sometimes, that's all it takes to get your gears in motion. Keep that in mind and give re-framing a try if you find yourself suck in the mud.

> ➤ **Try not to jump too far ahead of yourself.**
>
> In the past, I saw the road ahead of me as a path consisting of tasks, obstacles, obligations, and other barriers that all vied for my free time. Today, I now know that no matter what may lay head of me, I can only deal with one task at a time; so, I've learned to change my perspective. I only write down what I need to "do," and then I concentrate on just that one task, until it's been completed. And while I'm at work on that task, I try not to burden my mind with other concerns, because I've found the more I concentrate on a task, the quicker it generally goes, with less chance of making an error along the way of completing it.

> ➤ **Learn to laugh at troublesome situations.**
>
> Sometimes, when I feel under pressure, if I feel like saying to myself, "How did I get into this situation?", I counter that thought by comically saying to myself, "Poor old Dave!" I've found that if I look for the absurd in a situation, it helps me snap out of self-centeredness and self-pity, and it puts me back in the larger world. Try it yourself.

> ➤ **Develop a positive attitude by catching yourself when you're being a pessimist.**
>
> Habitual procrastinators are often habitual pessimists too. Avoid the habit of expecting and predicting the worst in every situation you find yourself in. If you need to, sit down with pen and paper and draw a simple chart with two columns. In the left column, write down all the negatives that you're facing, like "I don't want to do this," and then in the right column, write down some positive aspects of the situation. Force yourself to think differently, even if you can only find one positive attribute, such as "I'll sure be glad when I've finished this task." Then, concentrate on that positive attribute and finish the task.

> ➢ **Try not to compare yourself to others.**
>
> This is especially apt when it comes to your colleagues in the workplace. Avoid making self-statements like, "I can't do _____ as fast as (him) or (her)." We all have our own special talents, so avoid putting yourself down by being unnecessarily hard on yourself. Lastly, try not to "Compare and Despair."

Fight Panic Attacks With These Suggestions:

> ➢ **Calm yourself down by recalling a way that's worked for you in the past.**
>
> Go as far back in your mind as you need to, and find a situation where you pleasantly surprised yourself in how you dealt with a challenging task. If you can't come up with anything, then pretend that you're conducting a job interview with a mirror image of yourself as the applicant, and ask that mirror image to tell you about such a time. Then sit back and listen to yourself.

> ➢ **Stop panic by engaging in positive self-talk.**
>
> Engage in sensible self-talk by reminding yourself that you don't need to do everything at once. Retake control of your attitude by forcing yourself to look at individual tasks rather than at a messy apartment or a cluttered e-mail In-box. Then tell yourself: "All I need to do right now is to deal with just one item."
>
> One morning I awoke to the familiar cavalcade of regret and worry that made up my panic attacks, but then I reminded myself of the housework that I had done the previous night. The memory of my productivity pierced the fog and haze of that morning's attack like the beacon from a lighthouse. My panic attack then began fading, all because I put the memory of my previous day's productivity to practical use.

> ➢ **If your life feels like it's out of control.**
>
> Sometimes, it's more important to get just one task done, if only to disprove your irrational belief that you're an incapable person. So get something done, because that first completed task will be like a small snowball that when rolled around and around, eventually creates a tremendous snowball. In the same exact way, after you've handled a bunch of tasks, you'll soon feel pride in your newfound abilities!

> ➤ **Tell yourself, "I'm O.K. I'm not in danger."**
>
> Going through a panic attack is like being in a building where a loud fire alarm has gone off, but after the firefighters show up, they discover the alarm is faulty. Unfortunately, they can't shut it off, so it continues to loudly shriek—despite the fact that there's no real danger.
>
> If you're approaching a task that you truly dislike, remind yourself that although you may not feel comfortable being in that particular situation, that you're O.K., and aren't in real danger. Continue telling yourself that and write it down if you need to. Then break your task down into a smaller component, write it on your J.O.T. list, and then act upon it.

When Depression Feels Immobilzing, Fight Back at It with These Rules:

> ➤ **Depression fighting Rule No. 1: Do not stay in bed!**
>
> Before going to sleep, set your alarm for a reasonable amount of time, and when it goes off, get out of bed, and then make your bed. If you want to have something for your J.O.T. list, put "make my bed immediately after getting up," as your first task to complete tomorrow—then "do" it, and draw a line through that first task of the day. You'll feel better for it. Not sure? Don't just take my word for it. Try it yourself and see what happens.

> ➤ **Depression fighting Rule No. 2: Do not crawl back into bed!**
>
> Once you're out of bed, stay out of it. If you are strong enough and only if you can safely do this, pull your mattress and box spring out of your bed's frame, and stand them against a wall. Then do the same with the frame. Afterwards, you can put those tasks down on your J.O.T. list and immediately strike a line through them. Warning: This may cause you to feel invigorated.

> ➤ **Depression fighting Rule No. 3: There's no better time to clean than when you're feeling depressed.**
>
> If you're suffering from a difficult bout of depression, know that this is an awesome time to clean. Dust a little, mop a little, organize some files, or alphabetize your collection of 12-inch disco re-mixes. Whatever it is, just keep on the move. Remember: "Move a muscle, change a thought!" All the while, don't forget to jot down everything that you're about to take action upon on your J.O.T. list.

> ➤ **Depression fighting Rule No. 4: Exercise!**
>
> As long as it's approved by your doctor, fight depression the natural way, with exercise. It doesn't need to be much, as long as you get your heart pumping blood to your brain. Push-ups are great at helping you fight depression because you can feel both your weight and gravity against your muscles. You only need to do a few of them, and you will feel better!

> ➤ **Depression fighting Rule No. 5: Know whom to call.**
>
> If you're really feeling down, don't be afraid to admit to someone else that you need help. Consult a psychiatrist or a trained therapist. Write down the telephone number of a crisis hotline, such as The Samaritans, and don't feel ashamed to call them. They're there to listen to you.

General Suggestions:

> ➤ **Sometimes I need to re-start my day.**
>
> We all have days when we seem to have gotten up on the wrong side of bed, days when nothing seems to go right. Luckily for us, we can always re-start our day whenever we want to.
>
> In order to do this, all you really need to do is to put the earlier part of the day behind you and to make a promise with yourself either to enjoy the rest of the day or to make it productive. Don't forget the first Golden Rule of Overcoming Procrastination: "Always keep the promises that you make with yourself."
>
> Of course, the best way to make the rest of the day enjoyable is to be productive, because then you'll have nothing to regret. Plus, you'll feel the warm glow that comes from accomplished tasks. So keep that promise, and enjoy the rest of your day.

> ➤ **Today's sacrifice equals tomorrow's success.**
>
> The concept of sacrifice is one that many habitual procrastinators and non-procrastinators alike tend not to consider.
>
> While the concept of sacrifice may have been lost to a great degree in today's "me, me, me" society, you can use it to your benefit, especially when you face tasks that are challenging, complicated, boring, or unpleasant. Here's how it works: if you can't bring yourself to face the task for your own reasons, then consider doing the task for someone else's benefit. For example, let's say that you hate filing your tax return. What are some valid reasons for making the sacrifice of dealing with this annual ritual?
>
> For example: Think for a moment of all the Internal Revenue Service workers who depend on receiving and processing your tax forms in order to earn a living. When you file your taxes, you're helping someone at the processing center to earn wages, and that's a very good reason for making the sacrifice of the time and energy that you spend in filing out your return.
>
> Finally, perhaps the best reason for making a sacrifice is to experience the positive feeling that you'll receive from taking care of yourself. All that sitting down and tallying up of figures, the filling in of those governmental forms with their check boxes and signature lines; they all turn out to be worth "do"-ing after all!
>
> For persons like ourselves, it's not only the best reason for accomplishing any task, but it's especially true when it pertains to a task that we particularly dislike. Remember: "Every task has a silver lining."

> ➤ **The greater the task, the greater the benefit.**
>
> As procrastinators, we're quick to think that the greater the task, the greater the cost. We developed that way of thinking because we felt we had too much at stake to lose. We fear that dealing with tasks means losing our free time, and so, our independence.
>
> However, as you grow into a true non-procrastinator, you'll notice that you not only regain your free time, but you'll also restore your perspective, your patience, and your self-esteem, which combined: take the form of an overall feeling of well being.
>
> Soon you'll find that the more you "do," the more you're capable of, and as we "do," we build up our internal reservoir of strength, which makes us even stronger.

Setbacks and The J.O.T. Method™

The J.O.T. Method™ is only a means to an end. We want to end our procrastinating ways, and The J.O.T. Method™ helps us to achieve that overall goal. However, just as nobody's perfect, no one method of anything can be perfect either. If you've experienced any difficulties in adjusting to The J.O.T. Method™, go over the following points. They may be the help that you've been looking for:

> ➤ **Feel good about yourself while you're becoming acclimated to The J.O.T. Method™.**
>
> As you may have already read, habitual procrastinators aren't just people who have grown accustomed to not "do"-ing, they're also people who share many behavioral characteristics and traits. Two traits that come up repeatedly are frustration and impatience.
>
> These two traits cause us to feel flustered and drained of energy whenever we feel challenged, and this can hamper the process of changing from a procrastinator into a "do"-er. However, remember that there is an antidote to frustration and impatience you can employ to propel yourself forward in overcoming the thief of time that is procrastination: that antidote is willingness, because you must willingly give yourself permission to deal with your tasks.
>
> You've waged battle against personal responsibility for such a long time, you're probably wondering if the war is really over. What's more, you've fought for so long that you're probably much better at fighting your tasks than you are at making peace with them. That's why willingness is so crucially necessary if one is to truly win the war you've been waging against yourself.
>
> In time, you'll see an improvement in your ability to handle chores, no matter how unpleasant they may be, or may have been in the past. Overcoming procrastination means living life on life's terms, and that means dealing with one task at a time—to the best of present capability. In time, you'll be amazed at your success. Just give yourself the willingness to go through the process.

> ➤ **Don't create an overly long "to-do" list.**
>
> You may feel a certain temptation to walk around your living space with your notebook in hand, writing down every little task that you see. However, be cautious. We procrastinators are great at making "to-do" lists: I know, because I used to have several "to-do" lists perched on my kitchen table at any given time. However, the principle of The J.O.T. Method™ isn't to see how many tasks you can write down; it's actually to deal with each task immediately after having jotted it down.
>
> The trick is to only give yourself one task to "do"—remember, the letters J.O.T. stand for "just **one** task." So if things haven't gone well for you, throw out your current J.O.T. list, and start writing a new one. You can even make your new list's first task: "T/O old J.O.T. list." Then toss your old list in the trash, and put a line through that first task to make it look like this: ~~"T/O old J.O.T. list."~~ Then, continue on with your new list.

➢ **Never put a line through a task unless the action has been completed.**

I developed The J.O.T. Method™ as a way of dealing with my own habitual procrastination, and as I used the technique, I soon discovered that if I strayed from its simplicity, I got into trouble using it. For example, there were times when I jotted down a very minor task, and since I wanted to save time, I'd put a line through that task the moment after I'd written it. Unfortunately, doing that has the unintentional side-effect of sabotaging the method because even if a task seems insignificant, accomplishing it and then rewarding yourself by putting that line through it afterwards is enormously important to us because that line formally and properly draws a conclusion to that task. And it's a conclusion that we can look back upon again and again.

Moreover, it's crucial to focus at first on the simplest tasks that you can find, because in all probability, the easier the task, the quicker it will get done. However, what I've found from my own experience is that after having accomplished fifteen or more relatively simple tasks, I would occasionally grow overconfident, and begin writing tasks with the completion line already through them before I had actually dealt with them. After a little while longer, I'd look at my list and see something like twenty completed tasks, and I'd feel confused and I'd start making negative self-statements, like: "Which one's haven't I done? Why haven't I done these yet? I've screwed up somehow. I've got so much to get done! I'm such an idiot!"

What we don't want is for you to become overwhelmed, which is exactly what happened to me. Instead, we need to approach each and every task as an individual item, and that means finding a task that needs "do"-ing, writing it down on your J.O.T. list, accomplishing the task, and then, and only then, putting a line through that entry.

➢ **Always do a complete action.**

Whenever you engage in a task that you've written on your J.O.T. list, always make certain that the task is "do"-able as you've written it. If the task doesn't seem "do"-able, then stop for a moment, rethink it, and re-write it if you need to, following the directions that appear in Chapter 11 in the section entitled "How to Rewrite a Task."

> ➤ **Always draw a line through a task after it has been completed.**

There may be times when you won't feel like putting a line through a task on your J.O.T. list that you've just completed. This may happen because you felt like you were on a roll, so you plunged right into your next task. This often occurs when the tasks that you are doing are very simple in nature, like getting rid of things that you know have little value, such as expired coupons and unsolicited junk mail.

However, there are good reasons for following The J.O.T. Method™ and one of them is to develop the rhythm of "do"-ing. This is because after you've used the method numerous times, you won't need to think to yourself, "What do I do now?" or, "What do I do next?"

As previously mentioned, many habitual procrastinators become overwhelmed by their tasks quite easily; in fact, many need only think of the tasks that await them, and they may feel panicky. That, in turn, can result in producing a feeling of panic within you, which may make you feel like giving up on pursuing your tasks. After all, one of the prime reasons why many of us have become habitual procrastinators is because when we feel that panic, we take that feeling as if it were a signal from our bodies telling us to stay away from the things that upset us. So, the last thing we want to do is to set off a false alarm in our faulty nervous systems. Luckily, the best way to avoid doing that is easy: all you need to do is follow along with The J.O.T. Method™ step-by-step, keeping on track with each task from the moment that you've jotted it down in your notebook, until you've drawn a line through it upon its completion.

Remember too that every time you draw a line through a task, you're silently telling yourself, "Yes! I did it!" this will give you a sense of accomplishment each and every time that you put that line through a completed task. You might say that "do"-ing and then putting a line through the corresponding task is like killing two birds with one stone, because you've completed a task, which is fantastic, and you're rewarding yourself for a well-done endeavor. Don't deny yourself that reward: stop all activity for a moment, look at the task that you've just completed, draw that line, and feel good about what you've done.

If you consistently use The J.O.T. Method™ as suggested, you will have consistent results. So force yourself to keep to The J.O.T. Method's simple formula for overcoming habitual procrastination.

> ➤ **Do not be concerned over how long a task may take.**
>
> Even the simplest task that can no longer be broken down into smaller steps will sometimes take longer than expected. In addition, we may sometimes be resistant to dealing with a particular task: for more on this, return to the section, "Many Procrastinators Feel Frustrated When They Return To An Abandoned Task," which is featured in Chapter Four.
>
> Needless to say, the best course of action to take—is to take action. Allow a task to have its way with time. If a task is taking longer than you had planned, do as much as you can do and then transfer the remainder to your next day's J.O.T. list. Don't see this as a setback—instead, see it as a *fallback,* because you now have something to "do" tomorrow.
>
> Then, when tomorrow arrives, you won't need to worry, "What should I take care of first?" All you'll need to do is to look at your J.O.T. list and you'll have the answer.
>
> ➤ **When life happens.**
>
> Life sometimes gets in the way of even the best non-procrastinator; that's just the way life is. However, although events may cause you to detour from your plans, it's comforting to know that if you're forced to veer off track for a few hours or even for a few days, you can always refer back to your J.O.T. list, which is your roadmap.
>
> I recall a great piece of advice a friend once gave me, "Plan your work—and work your plan." I still follow that advice to this day.

Lastly, here's a table that contains a comparison of two different scenarios. Which scenario do you prefer?

How Can You Expect To Feel Good?	Why Wouldn't You Feel Great?
➤ You didn't complete any tasks for yourself last night after you came home from work, where you "do" for others.	➤ Last night after coming home from work where you "do" for others, you got a few chores out of the way. Now you'll have more free time over the weekend.

➢ You stayed up far too late last night, which made you feel like you're not in charge of your own life.	➢ You got to bed at a reasonable hour last night, because the tasks you completed during the evening made you feel like you had earned a pleasant night's rest.
➢ You woke up late this morning, which also made you feel like you weren't in control of your life.	➢ This morning, you awakened a few minutes before your alarm clock was set to ring. You felt calm after a satisfying night's rest.
➢ You didn't complete any tasks for yourself before going to work, where you "do" for others. As a result, you felt like you didn't serve any purpose, other than "do"-ing for others.	➢ Before heading off to work, you took care of some light housekeeping chores because you felt like "do"-ing for yourself before "do"-ing for others at work. It's just as well, because you like the feeling of coming back to a tidy home after a day of work.
➢ You didn't exercise today, which made you feel tired and sluggish. In fact, you had such an overall downer of a day; you didn't feel like you had enough energy to exercise.	➢ After work, you dropped in at the health club, pumped a bit of iron, and ran a couple of miles on a treadmill, just to get your blood flowing. You feel great.
➢ You feel drawn out and would like to crawl under a rock, if only you could. So then, how's tomorrow looking to you?	➢ You feel warm, strong, and satisfied. So then, how's tomorrow looking to you?

In short, the scenario that you find yourself in tomorrow will be based on the decisions that you make today.

Chapter Thirteen

Advanced Techniques for Overcoming Procrastination

I AM OCCASIONALLY ASKED WHETHER I ever engage in procrastination? It's only fair that I get asked that, and the answer to it is—only on the rarest occasions. You see, I've now become so used to taking care of my responsibilities that to deliberately delay acting upon a task would be to go against my newfound nature.

However, there's an another reason of even greater importance that makes it quite difficult for me to evade my tasks, and that's because of the connection that I've found between procrastination and depression. I have learned through first hand experience that the decisions I make today—will determine how I'll feel tomorrow. It seems that no matter which angle that I look at this from, this concept always holds true. As long as I place my concern today, for how I'll feel tomorrow, I know that I will act accordingly. After all, if I put a task off by finding a distraction, I'm still going to have to face that task tomorrow, when I'll again need to make a decision on whether to deal with it, or to avoid it once more.

In the past, I thought I was putting off my tasks for another day, a day when I'd feel more up to them. Today, I know differently. I'm now aware that if I deliberately put off a task today, I'll not only be less likely to deal with it tomorrow, but I'll also feel poorer for that decision. And, if I continue putting that task off, I'll soon begin wondering if I'm less capable, or *less than*, other adults. Today, thankfully, I know I wouldn't want to put myself in a bind like that again. Been there, done that.

So, while I could procrastinate if I really wanted to, it simply wouldn't justify all of the sadness, anxiety, low self-esteem, negative self-talk, and loss of energy from depression that I'd go through the following day, or longer. And that's too high a price to pay for what was otherwise supposed to have been an act of pressure relief.

Life Today

The way I live today is remarkably different from the way I lived in the past. For example, upon returning home after withdrawing money from an automatic teller machine, there's a positive force that's present in my life that makes me remove the transaction slip from my wallet which prevents me from carrying it around for several days while my checkbook remains unbalanced. While I might not enter the transaction into my checkbook the very minute I arrive home, that positive force simply will not allow that transaction slip to linger on my kitchen table in the same way that I once would have allowed it to. That force is *the force of positive habits,* which has replaced the force of negative habits, which had pretty much ruled and determined my existence.

The same is true concerning other household chores. Dishes and silverware no longer accumulate in my sink—not because I've become overly fastidious about cleanliness, but because I've developed the positive habit of washing the utensils I used to prepare my meal, either while the food is still cooking, or just before I sit down to eat. And, after I've finished eating, it no longer seems to make sense to leave dirty dishes in the sink without first washing them. That doesn't mean that I've become a perfectionist, far from it, because I will leave dirty dishes in the sink if I don't have any other options; for example, if I need to go somewhere immediately after eating, then I go. However, I know that when I arrive back home, I'll only have a few dirty items that require my attention because many of the items I had used to prepare my meal had already been washed before I sat down to eat. If you haven't already read the section "Science Experiments in the Kitchen," then I invite you to read through it in Chapter One in order to properly contrast the person that I am today from the person that I was a few years ago.

After putting an end to my habitual procrastination, I took the next step and became a non-procrastinator. Just to be clear, that doesn't mean I never procrastinate, or that I will never procrastinate ever again. Rather, I began acting like the kind of person who isn't all that troubled if they happen to procrastinate on something, because they engage in it so rarely, that it's hardly consequential in their life. In addition, as I previously mentioned at the start of this chapter, the price that I would have to pay for engaging in procrastination is so high that it never seems worth the risk of the downside.

It's important to point out that the changes that I have undergone have been gradual, and have taken place over a long time span. If you've just become acquainted with The J.O.T. Method™ and have recently begun working on your own issues with procrastination, be aware that there's no need to immediately delve into these advanced techniques, because the last thing you want to do is put yourself under any unnecessary pressure. What's more, remember that you can always come back to this chapter whenever you feel ready to improve upon your productivity.

So then, what improvements did I find? First, over time, I improved my overall productivity by creating a couple of enhancements to The J.O.T. Method™. Then, I found a different relationship to "do"-ing, which involved becoming comfortable with tasks that required greater amounts of time to complete. And lastly, I found some additional aids to productivity that had less to do with an orderly procedure like The J.O.T. Method™, and much more to do with how I developed an attitude of orderliness within myself.

Improvements on The J.O.T. Method™

If you've mastered the basics of The J.O.T. Method™ and are ready to take your next steps in reducing the role procrastination plays in your life, consider two improvements to it that may facilitate your "do"-ing. The first improvement can help you to reduce the amount of time that you spend writing your J.O.T. list by combining similar items that you've accomplished, while the second improvement is geared towards increasing your motivation.

The Combining Technique

Let's say that Barry, whom you met in Chapters 10 and 11, has implemented The J.O.T. Method™ into his life and has been successfully using it to help him get his tasks done. Six months have passed since Barry first started using The J.O.T. Method™. Let's look at Barry's most recent J.O.T. list entry:

Saturday, September 8th

~~G/B Jessie Chang~~
~~T/O old newspaper~~
~~T/O old newspaper~~
~~dust bookshelves~~
~~Mop floors~~
~~T/O old newspaper~~
~~P/A business card~~
~~P/A health club flyer~~
~~L/M Geoff's telephone number~~
~~G/T newspaper clipping~~
~~Fix radiator cover~~
~~T/O newspaper clipping~~
~~Clean kitchen chair~~
~~Clean kitchen chair~~
~~Clean kitchen chair~~
~~Clean kitchen chair~~
~~Play pinball on computer 20 mins.~~
~~T/O old magazine~~
~~P/A take out menu~~
~~P/A telephone calling card~~

~~P/A business card~~
~~P/A business card~~
~~T/O old newspaper~~
~~T/O old newspaper~~
~~L/M Louie Wheelman~~
~~Fill out gym membership form~~
~~Run defrag on computer~~
~~P/A business card~~
~~Start list of groceries needed~~
~~T/O old newspaper~~
~~T/O old magazine~~
~~Update computer anti-virus~~
~~Run computer anti-virus scan~~
~~T/O junk mail item~~
Shop for groceries

Not only can we readily see that Barry has had a very productive Saturday, but we can also see that he has completed a variety of tasks. In order to keep things moving, Barry sometimes completes two tasks of the exact same type in a row, while at other times he mixes things up by completing a task of one type, and then following it by completing a task of a different nature.

By juggling things in this way, Barry keeps things moving and he averts the risk of becoming overwhelmed by anxiety or bored by monotony. Notice as well, the item in his J.O.T. list's first column, showing that Barry even allowed himself to play pinball on his computer for twenty minutes. You might say it was a "pre-planned break." So long as Barry returns to his work once his break has run its course, there's no reason why he shouldn't enjoy a reasonable intermission from his tasks. While playing pinball isn't a task in the traditional sense, it still merits being placed on his J.O.T. list because in time, upon review of his notebook, Barry will have a clearer picture as to what activities he chose, and the order in which they were performed on that particular Saturday.

We can also see that in the second column of his J.O.T. list, Barry's written, "Start list of groceries needed," which is then followed by six tasks, and ends with "Shop for groceries." It's not particularly difficult to imagine that just after Barry started writing his grocery list on a separate sheet of paper, he then began completing additional tasks in conjunction with his J.O.T. list. It only follows that while he was working on those tasks, he was probably thinking of what he needed from the supermarket, and would then write those items down while switching between working on the grocery list and whichever task was at hand. Lastly, just before leaving home to go shopping, Barry completed his last task, "T/O (throw out) junk mail item," which he then officially completed by drawing a line through its appearance on his J.O.T. list. Below that we can see, "Shop for groceries," and since no line has been drawn through it, it's probably safe to say that Barry is at the supermarket right now.

So, by creating his grocery list while he was engaged in other chores, Barry maximized his time while anticipating his future needs. Even better, by occasionally thinking of what he needed from the supermarket, Barry not only kept busy with his chores, he also made things a tad more lively for himself.

While Barry knows that the letters "J.O.T." stand for "Just One Task," he also knows that he's grown a great deal over the last six months. Even now, Barry feels capable of handling a bit more than he could only a few weeks ago. This explains why Barry is able to work on his grocery list, while tending to the tasks that he already wrote on his J.O.T. list. Although this is not something that he does each and every day, the more that Barry accomplishes, the stronger he feels—which just happens to be the complete opposite of the very last characteristic of procrastination listed in Chapter Four: "As Procrastination Grows Stronger—The Procrastinator Feels Weaker!" It's safe to say that Barry has come a long way.

While we've seen that Barry has gotten a great deal done, there is an alternate way he could have created his J.O.T. list, one that could speed him along his way as far as writing is concerned, by combining similar items. With this alternate process, The J.O.T. Method™ is performed in the same way as before—the only change is in how it's written.

In order for you to make use of this alternate J.O.T. writing method, you will need the following conditions present:

1. You need to have a good number of tasks that need attention.
2. Many of those tasks need to be exactly alike—for example, you have many books to place on a shelf, or you have a lot of CDs to arrange.
3. You have a good amount of free time available that you're willing to devote to these tasks.

Let's look again at the J.O.T. list that Barry wrote for Saturday, September 8th:

Saturday, September 8th

[G/B Jessie Chang]
T/O old newspaper
T/O old newspaper
dust bookshelves
Mop floors
T/O old newspaper
P/A business card
P/A health club flyer
L/H Geoff's telephone number
G/T newspaper clipping
Fix radiator cover
T/O newspaper clipping
Clean kitchen chair
Clean kitchen chair
Clean kitchen chair
Clean kitchen chair
Play pinball on computer 20 mins.
T/O old magazine
P/A take out menu
P/A telephone calling card

P/A business card
P/A business card
T/O old newspaper
T/O old newspaper
L/M Louie Wheelman
Fill out gym membership form
Run defrag on computer
P/A business card
Start list of groceries needed
T/O old newspaper
T/O old magazine
Update computer anti-virus
Run computer anti-virus scan
T/O junk mail item
Shop for groceries

As we can gather from analyzing his J.O.T. list, Barry had accumulated many newspapers and magazines, and he had plenty of business cards to file away. While he accomplished a great deal, which is something that Barry should be very happy about, much of it involved the same items being written many times over on his J.O.T. list.

If Barry wrote each item only once and substituted vertical "ditto" marks for each similar task, he would have more room for other tasks, and he wouldn't need to spend time thinking about each item as he wrote them down. In addition, Barry could increase his productivity as a result of his spending a bit less time writing out each and every one of his tasks.

Here's what Barry's J.O.T. list would have looked like if he had combined similar items:

Saturday, September 8th

{C/B Jessie Chang}
T/O old newspaper |||||
dust bookshelves
Mop floors
P/A business card |||
P/A health club flyer
L/U Geoff's telephone number
G/T newspaper clipping
Fix radiator cover
T/O newspaper clipping
Clean kitchen chair |||
Play pinball on computer 20 mins.
T/O old magazine |
P/A take out menu
P/A telephone calling card
L/U Louie Wheelman
Fill out gym membership form
Run defrag on computer
Start list of groceries needed

Update computer anti-virus
Run computer anti-virus scan
T/O junk mail item
Shop for groceries

As you can see, this alternate process has the effect of streamlining Barry's J.O.T. list by economizing space within the list, allowing more room for future tasks and leaving his J.O.T. list looking less cluttered. Of course, some people might prefer the traditional J.O.T. list, and if the traditional J.O.T. list works for you, then feel free to stick with it.

The Counting Technique

Our second improvement on The J.O.T. Method™ may help you increase your level of motivation with regard to your tasks.

There may come a time when you've spent the greater part of a Saturday or Sunday taking care of little chores around the house. After having climbed Mount Paperwork, you might feel slightly lightheaded—not from altitude sickness, but from the mixed feeling you get that's part elation at how much you've gotten done, and part tiredness from of the hard work you engaged in. It's at this particular point that you'll need to make a decision on whether to:

➢ Carry on and "do" more.
➢ Take a break.
➢ Or to call it a day.

As a recovering procrastinator, you may have faced a particular problem many of us have also experienced. It concerns our practice of taking a break, but not resuming work after that break should have ended. The best way to avoid encountering this problem is to avoid taking unnecessary breaks. Notice that I specifically referred to "unnecessary breaks." While we want to avoid taking unnecessary breaks because they can affect our productivity, we always need to preserve our right to take breaks when we truly need them. We never want to overwork ourselves, because that could backfire on fire on us by depleting our reserves of mental and/or physical energy, which might then make us feel panicked and overwhelmed. For people like us, that's a recipe for disaster. As long as you keep that in mind, you should be all right.

That said, there may be times when you'll find yourself wanting to continue working, while also wanting to take a break, and it's at those times that a little motivation might help maintain your forward momentum. Fortunately, one of the most effective ways to keep going also happens to have one of the simplest solutions. All you need to do is count the number of tasks that you've completed, and then jot that number down to the right of the last task you've completed on your J.O.T. list. The only rule that must be followed in order for this to work is that you must write that number down **before** taking your break. What often happens as a result of practicing this simple technique is that whatever number of completed tasks that you have calculated, there's a part of human nature within you that will likely ask, "Could that number be just a little higher? Could I squeeze in one more task before my break?"

Using the same J.O.T. list as we did at the start of this chapter, let's compare The Counting Technique to the traditional version of The J.O.T. Method™. In this example, all Barry needs to do is count his completed tasks, look over the last number written, and see if he feels up to raising the count. Let's see how Barry used this simple technique. Reverting to Barry's last J.O.T. list without the streamlining that came from The Combining Technique, Barry's J.O.T. list now looks like this:

<u>Saturday, September 8th</u>

[C/B Jessie Chang]

T/O old newspaper

T/O old newspaper

dust bookshelves

Mop floors

T/O old newspaper

P/A business card

P/A health club flyer

L/U Geoff's telephone number

G/T newspaper clipping

Fix radiator cover

T/O newspaper clipping

Clean kitchen chair

Clean kitchen chair

Clean kitchen chair

Clean kitchen chair

Play pinball on computer 20 mins.

T/O old magazine

P/A take out menu

P/A telephone calling card

P/A business card

P/A business card

T/O old newspaper

T/O old newspaper

L/M Louie Wheelman

Fill out gym membership form

Run defrag on computer

P/A business card

Start list of groceries needed

T/O old newspaper

T/O old magazine

Update computer anti-virus

Run computer anti-virus scan

T/O junk mail item

Shop for groceries

Put groceries away

As you may have noticed, Barry's J.O.T. list tells us that he's come back from shopping and he's put his groceries away, because he's struck a line through those tasks. Barry now finds himself wondering whether he's up for more tasks. While he wants to get *more* done, after looking over his J.O.T. list, he's found that although it confirms his productivity, it didn't tell him *exactly* how productive he had been. In order to motivate himself, Barry practiced "The Counting Technique."

First, he began counting the number of tasks he had completed, writing every tenth number to the side of that task. "Ten…, twenty…, thirty." Then he counted up the last tasks he had accomplished, "Thirty-four…, thirty-five…, thirty-six!" and he wrote that number to the side of his last completed task. Here's what Barry's J.O.T. list looked like after he copied those numbers to his J.O.T. list:

Saturday, September 8th

[C/B Jessie Chang]	P/A business card
T/O old newspaper	P/A business card
T/O old newspaper	T/O old newspaper
dust bookshelves	T/O old newspaper
Mop floors	L/M Louie Wheelman
T/O old newspaper	Fill out gym membership form
P/A business card	Run defrag on computer
P/A health club flyer	P/A business card
L/M Geoff's telephone number	Start list of groceries needed
G/T newspaper clipping 10	T/O old newspaper 30
Fix radiator cover	T/O old magazine
T/O newspaper clipping	Update computer anti-virus
Clean kitchen chair	Run computer anti-virus scan
Clean kitchen chair	T/O junk mail item
Clean kitchen chair	Shop for groceries
Clean kitchen chair	Put groceries away 36
Play pinball on computer 20 mins.	
T/O old magazine	
P/A take out menu	
P/A telephone calling card 20	

Almost instantly, Barry's mind began to ponder: "Hmm… I wonder if I could get 40 tasks done? That's a nice round number. There are a few other small chores that I could get done. They wouldn't take very long, and they wouldn't require a lot of physical or mental energy. Maybe I could just try doing one of them. Then I'd know that I had 36 tasks done. I'm sure if I went from 35 to 36, I'd almost definitely want to hit 40!"

The Counting Technique has other advantages too, because having numbers written down in your J.O.T. list from previous days can actually help motivate you in the future. It's only natural that one day you might flip through the pages of your notebook, and review how productive you were one week ago, one month ago, or on a particular day, and wonder if you could out-"do" yourself. So, your written J.O.T. record can become even more useful to you over the long run, because it not only shows you how productive you've been in the past, but at the same time, it can also help motivate you to keep going in the present.

You can also simultaneously use both of the improvements to The J.O.T. Method™ that you were introduced to in this section. The most important thing is to find the process that works for you. If you've found that the traditional way of using The J.O.T. Method™ makes you happy and productive, there's no reason to change gears.

After a while, you might even find your own way of customizing The J.O.T. Method™ that fits you to a tee. If that happens, then I warmly invite you to contact me via my web site, to let me know about your discovery.

Dealing With Larger Projects

There are some tasks that almost seem to take on a life of their own. They can exasperate and frustrate us, defy completion, and put up such a fight that we can feel as if we've caught a fish that's not only fighting back, but trying to snap the fishing line as well. While smaller tasks usually can be accomplished with the assistance of The J.O.T. Method™, there are some larger tasks that can swamp our physical and/or our emotional resources. Here are a few examples of these kinds of tasks:

> ➢ Starting a new business.

> ➢ Building an extension onto your home.

> ➢ Preparing for a major life event, like planning a large family wedding, or relocating.

I can tell you from first-hand experience that another unwieldy task that can exert a toll on someone is the writing and production of a book. After all, a book is not a "just one task" kind of chore; it's a project that's made up of thousands of concepts and ideas that must be coalesced into words, pages, and chapters. Plus, there are also the challenges getting the manuscript edited, having the book printed, sending word of the book out to the world, and then placing it into the hands of readers like yourself. As recovering procrastinators, we have enough difficulty just getting our smaller tasks done: so what do we do when a larger task or project threatens to exceed our ability to complete it?

The best way that I have found to deal with what seems like an unmanageable task is to compartmentalize my time, and deal with only one task for a specific time period in what I called a "timed event." This is different from The J.O.T. Method™, whereby we either take care of simple tasks, or we break down medium-sized tasks into their smaller, "do"-able components, which we then accomplish. Instead, when you create a timed event, you dedicate yourself to dealing with only one task for whatever period of time that you've allocated. The important thing is not to overwhelm yourself by devoting too much time to a task because that could make you feel trapped or like you need to escape, which is an old trait from your days as a habitual procrastinator.

Someone once said, "What gets measured, gets done." Any project that takes a good amount of time can always be measured in time, even future time. When you're confronted with a large project, it may be helpful to first try analyzing it in terms of how long it may take to complete. Even if the figure that you come up with is purely a guess, it's always good to think about how much time your project may take because by doing so, you're preparing yourself for the job ahead.

In order to size-up a large project, the following outline may be helpful:

1. Have your calendar handy and determine the timeframe by which you would like to have the project completed. Sometimes that timeframe will be dictated by the project. For example, there may be an external deadline that you need to have the project finished by, such as a date when forms must be completed, or a mailing envelope must be postmarked. If that's the case, then you'll need to know what that date is. It's also a good idea to mark that date on your calendar. If there isn't an external deadline, then your timeframe is simply the date that you'd like to have your project completed by.

2. To the best of your ability, estimate how much time you believe you project will take to complete, and then write that figure in your notebook expressed in minutes and/or hours. This may not be easy to do the first time you try it, but that's okay, just do the best you can. You don't need to be perfect, and your figure doesn't need to be perfect either—you just want to establish an estimate so you can get an understanding of what you're about to deal with.

3. Most importantly, avoid the trap of making vague or defeating self-statements like, "It's going to take forever!" or "I can't see how it's going to take anything less than several months." Statements like those are the complete opposite of what you want to come up with.

4. One good way to estimate time is by generalizing at first, and then working at developing a round figure that expresses how many hours the project might take to complete. For example, let's say that you look over your project and fairly estimate that it may take five weeks to complete. Furthermore, let's also say that your five-week estimate safely falls within any external deadline.

5. The next thing you'll want to do is to think about how much time you'd be willing to devote to your project over that five-week time span. Depending on how much free time you have, you could come up with a schedule like one hour during any three evenings of the workweek, and three hours every Saturday. This would come out to three evening hours each workweek, plus three hours each Saturday, which comes to an estimated six hours spent on the project each week. Since you previously estimated that you'd like to have the project completed within five weeks, all you need to do now is to multiply six hours per week times five weeks, which comes out to an estimate of thirty hours for the completion of the project.

6. As long as you have your calendar nearby, you might want to go over the weeks ahead. See whatever you already have planned and work your project into the calendar. Bear in mind that you only produced an estimate with round numbers, and you can always tailor your work to fit your personal schedule.

> 7. Remember as well, that by filling in your calendar with project reminders you're helping yourself to remain focused on your project, and to stay on track in regard to its deadline.

When your calendar and watch indicate that the time for working on your project has arrived, remember that you only need to work for the period of time that you've set aside. Once you've begun working on your timed event, use a stopwatch, or if you don't have a stopwatch, then write down the actual time in your notebook. Whichever way you time yourself, be sure to stop the clock for breaks, or deduct break time from your written total; and bear in mind that these are called *timed events* for a reason, so keep track of your time. Try not to do less that you promised yourself, and remember as always, The First Golden Rule of Overcoming Procrastination: "Always keep the promises that you make with yourself."

You may occasionally feel the temptation to do more by going beyond the amount of time that you've set aside. While you can always do this, it's important to point out that the only way that you're going to discover that you've gone too far beyond your limits is when you find that you've exhausted yourself. This is something that you do **not** want to do, because when your next calendar date for working on the project comes around you do not want to be put off by the bad memory of your most recent experience. Remember that too much of anything is not a good thing, and this is especially true when it applies to overworking ourselves; so, at least for now, try sticking to the plan at hand. While our goal has always been to overcome habitual procrastination, our goal has never been to set world records in productivity, especially with regard to lengthy projects. This is the reason why we map out our timeframes, and use the calendar and clock as well.

If you run into any difficulties while working on your project, remember that you always have The J.O.T. Method™ at your disposal. Use it to break any larger-sized tasks into more manageable units. You'll also want to keep track of your project in your notebook, whether by using The J.O.T. Method™, or simply by writing down what you've been doing and calculating how much time you've accumulated while working on that project.

Here are some additional suggestions regarding timed events:

> ➤ If you have any problems getting a timed event underway, start off the easy way by working in ten-minute time units. After you've gotten your first ten minutes of work done, take a deep breath, make a note of the time, and start working on another ten-minute unit.

> ➤ Be realistic. A big job is going to take time and effort, so give yourself time to grow comfortable with the idea of methodically working on a big project.

> ➤ When you work on a project, work slowly and in an orderly manner, and resist any temptation to rush things.

> ➤ Find the little joys that a big project has to offer and don't be afraid of actually enjoying yourself. You may find a special sense of security in the knowledge that you always have the option of having something more constructive to do than watching television.

> ➤ Consider making a game out of your work whenever you can.

> ➤ Be amazed by how much work you can get done in just ten or fifteen minutes, when comparing that to how much time you used to waste by watching television for thirty- or sixty-minute intervals.

> ➤ Discover the power that you now have to start working on long-term projects, along with your ability to stop working, and then being able to pick up working once again. Compare that to how you used to behave as a habitual procrastinator, and learn to appreciate your new abilities.

> ➤ Look at the passing of time on your stopwatch as you work as a boost to your self-esteem and be proud that you're now taking better care of yourself than you did as a procrastinator.

The following advanced techniques for overcoming procrastination have more to do with what we can do in a physical sense to increase our personal productivity:

Use Light Housecleaning as a Starter for Your More Difficult Tasks

Sometimes we see our projects as larger than life, and as a result, we feel immobilized in our tasks' shadows. One good solution that I've found to this feeling of immobilization is to engage in light housekeeping. I've found that it's a great starter-task that helps me prepare for my more challenging tasks.

The moment I get off from my couch and begin cleaning or organizing, I being feeling differently. Even if I'm only dampening a rag and running it around my bookshelves, I'm actually "do"-ing a lot more than just that because my mind becomes busy finding targets that require dusting, and then completing each action.

When I make it my mission to seek and destroy dusty surfaces, the "do"-er part of my mind perks up. In fact, it doesn't matter if I'm dusting, arranging photos in an album, or taking care of any other small task that I find, because the moment that I begin taking care of that task, I've also begun taking care of myself. As a result, not only do I begin feeling better about myself, I start feeling more capable as well. Just like the action of creating a snowball and making it larger and larger, when I make myself do minor tasks like mopping my floors, arranging my shoes, and tidying up my home, I'm not only preparing myself to "do" more, but to handle more too.

The Best Anti-Depressant I've Ever Found Has Been My Filing Cabinet

In the past, I envied people who had neat and organized homes. They seemed able to find almost anything instantly, whereas I had a difficult time finding things in just a small studio apartment.

You might not think there could be that many places where important papers could hide, but there were times when I would forage high and low for receipts, wage statements, owners manuals, and warranty cards.

During those frantic paper hunts, especially around tax time, there was an atmosphere you'd expect to find at a search for forensic evidence—no stone was left unturned. During those times that I would repeatedly ask myself:

> ➤ "Why did I put *that* there?"

> ➤ "What made me think that *that* was a good place to store something as important as *this?*"

> ➤ And, of course, "What was I *thinking?*"

By using a filing cabinet, you'll know where all your important papers are. Just think about how much more neat and organized your living space could be with the addition of a filing cabinet. Your home doesn't even need to take on the look of a business office, because many filing cabinets now come in different sizes, shapes and colors. As far as I'm concerned, because of all the organizational power and neatness that my filing cabinet has provided me with, I consider it the best anti-depressant I've ever found.

Develop a Mantra of "Patience"

Although the topic of developing a mantra using the word "Patience" was mentioned in the previous chapter, I believe that it's worth repeating in slightly expanded form because of the profound experience that I have had as a resulted of slowly chanting the word "patience" to myself.

We all have times when we encounter the feeling of frustration head-on. Sometimes frustration is like an ocean wave coming over us: there's nothing we can do except to prepare ourselves for it by turning our backs to the wave and letting it come over us. Frustration provides us with the perfect excuse for giving up on our tasks and calling it a day. However, I've found the one thing that almost always gives me a second wind: it's chanting the word "patience" to myself. Here's why it works:

> ➤ Chanting "patience" momentarily distracts me when I feel frustrated.

> ➤ Just as the thought of dealing with some tasks can get me bent out of shape for a few moments, I can just as easily calm myself down by chanting "patience" to myself.

> ➤ Shortly after I start chanting "patience," my mind regains its perspective. Once my frustration dissipates, I often begin thinking of a similar task that I accomplished in the past, and then I get down to business.

This method can work for you too: start out with "patience," or choose another calming word that will help you focus. Slowly chant your word to yourself a few times in a low voice, just as if it were a mantra. Speak slowly and calmly. Try this when you're frustrated, and see how it provides you with a few moments that you can use to refocus your mind back onto your task.

Here Are Some Additional Advanced Techniques for Overcoming Procrastination:

> ### ➢ Become Willing to Make Sacrifices
>
> Sometimes the only way that you can get a task done is by focusing all of your attention on it, and only it. There are times when I need to go all out, which means shutting off the radio or television, shutting all my lights, and then sitting at my desk with just a desk lamp lit above my workspace. There are times that I simply can't afford to have any distractions, and it's during those times when I need to be willing to make sacrifices—because in order to gain something, I need to be willing to give up something else.
>
> Luckily, after having changed from a habitual procrastinator into a non-procrastinator, you may not find it as easy to waste several hours in the same way that you once did. The thought of spending endless hours watching television may not seem as attractive as it did before your changeover. This is because you now feel a sense of responsibility towards yourself, as well as to others.
>
> Remember that whenever anyone wants to make a change, personal willingness makes all the difference; as long as you remain willing to make sacrifices, you'll have much more success in becoming the new you.
>
> ### ➢ Learn to Prioritize by Adopting an Attitude of "First Things First"
>
> What does "First Things First" mean? It means taking care of the most important need that you have first—with everything else coming in second place. Whenever you have a pressing task, take care of that task first, and everything else should be relatively easier, because less complicated tasks should require less mental and physical energy.
>
> Moreover, many of our second-place tasks are really just distractions that have more to do with escaping and floating than anything that might result in a well-earned accomplishment. When we adopt an attitude of "first things first," we put our needs ahead of our wants. Remember, by making something a priority—it becomes a priority.

➢ **Eliminate Conflicting Priorities By Deciding Which Task Has the Greatest Potential To Cause Depression**

When faced with conflicting priorities, many procrastinators prefer to go into shutdown mode, reverting to their alternate state of being by becoming Human Ostriches.

However, having come this far, you'll no longer want to go through that sort of reversal. Still, when faced with conflicting priorities, you may occasionally find yourself stuck in the mud. So, if you have several less than desirable tasks, how do you decide which task to deal with first?

I've found that what works best for me is to decide which task poses the largest risk of causing me depression. Whatever the other negatives might be, if one task has a higher potential to cause depression, then that key indicator tells me *that task* is *the one* that I must deal with first.

➢ **Think "Beginning and End"**

There are times when we only see a task as something that's large, formidable, and looming on the horizon, and it's at times like those that we may become prone to feeling overwhelmed.

Those are the times when it can be especially difficult to believe that the task ahead not only has a natural life span, but also has an end to its involvement with us. If you should ever lose that perspective about an approaching task, then challenge yourself to come up with a reasonable end to it. Be creative and write that ending down in your notebook, and always remind yourself that your task will not take forever. As long as you remember that your task has a definitive life span, you'll have a much easier time dealing with it.

➢ **Compromising Doesn't Need to Feel Compromising**

Sometimes when a habitual procrastinator finds himself faced with a difficult task that he'd rather not deal with, instead of finding a workable solution, he may decide to walk away from it by saying that he "doesn't want to make compromises." The procrastinator may see compromising as "giving in," something he might say is personally distasteful. While at first glance, the procrastinator may look like a principled person, his refusal to compromise is merely just one of the creative ways that his mind has come up with as a defense against the tasks he'd rather not deal with.

If this describes you, take heart in the fact that compromising doesn't necessarily mean "giving in," it's actually about coming to a decision, and that's what overcoming procrastination is all about: decision-making.

If you think about that for a moment, how could compromising be anything but a good decision? So, the next time you feel that must compromise in order to get something done, remember that compromising is really just the act of making a decision, much like any other decision that you might make.

➤ The Best Cure for the Worst Tasks

There are tasks, and then there are *tasks*. I can recall one time when I reluctantly agreed to an evening shift of transcribing a long audio recording. Transcription was something that I really didn't like; however, I needed to pay my rent and, not seeing a future in the field of bank robbery, I took the job. When I arrived at the office, I discovered that the transcription was not going to come from a secretarial audio playback unit, but from a common DVD player. While secretarial playback units are purpose-built with a foot switch and automatic tape reverse to give you a chance to see where you left off, I had no such luxuries and had to deal with what I had been given for that eight-hour shift.

I was faced with pressing the "Play" button with one hand and then getting that hand back on my keyboard as rapidly as possible in order to type a few quick words, only to then hit "Stop" and "Rewind," and then hope I had found the spot on the DVD where I had left off. As far as temp jobs went, this was "the job from hell."

Luckily, I had learned some time before that when I'm faced with a difficult task the best tactic is usually to work fast and accurately; and that's just what I did—I kept my head down and buried it in my work, and that tactic worked just fine. If you ever find yourself in a similar situation, remember that sometimes the only way out—is by moving forward.

➤ Reward Yourself for All the Hard Work You've Been Doing

Don't be afraid to reward yourself for all of the hard work that you've been doing. At this point, having an enjoyable break is something that you might want to start incorporating into your activities. In the past, we procrastinators would take a break and never return to our duties. While the thought our old ways of life may keep you on the straight and narrow, although that's well and good, you will eventually reach a point where a flat-out break is warranted.

Always remember that a restful break is different from goofing off. In addition, if you're concerned that when you take a break you'll have a difficult time returning to your tasks, then use an alarm clock to set a time for returning to your task, and make a promise with yourself to return to it when the alarm rings. I've found that one of the best rewards for my own hard work is placing my right hand atop my left shoulder and tapping that shoulder three or four times to say, "Well done." Find a reward that's meaningful to you, and use it as positive reinforcement when you complete your tasks.

Chapter Fourteen

The Procrastinator's Relationships with Significant Others

U P UNTIL NOW, OUR FOCAL point has almost exclusively been on the procrastinator's relationship with himself or herself, as he or she has been transformed from a habitual procrastinator into a non-procrastinator. We're going to depart from that slightly in this chapter as we look at people who interact closely with habitual procrastinators. In other words, we're going to take a look at what happens to people in interpersonal relationships with habitual procrastinators who haven't yet begun their transformations.

When someone who doesn't regularly procrastinate interacts with a habitual procrastinator, the non-procrastinator may feel frustrated by the behavior of the procrastinator. If the relationship between the two dictates that the non-procrastinator needs to depend upon the actions of the habitual procrastinator, such as when a non-procrastinating buyer agrees to purchase from a habitually procrastinating supplier who puts off replenishing his stock, the relationship can become strained. However, if the non-procrastinator and their procrastinating counterpart are in an even closer relationship, such as being married to each other, or if the non-procrastinator is the supervisor of a habitually procrastinating employee, the atmosphere between them can become downright combustible.

In order to examine these relationships, we'll first see how a habitual procrastinator might be viewed from the perspective of a non-procrastinating spouse, and later, by a non-procrastinating supervisor in the workplace.

The Habitual Procrastinator and His/Her Significant Other

Meet Colin, a frustrated non-procrastinator and Patricia, his glum procrastinating spouse. Part of the frustration that a non-procrastinating significant other like Colin commonly feels comes from his bewilderment at how his habitually procrastinating mate Patricia routinely goes about her tasks—or, perhaps more aptly, sprightly dances around them. For while Colin has lived his adult life in accord with mottoes such as "make hay while the sun shines," or "a stitch in time saves nine," he's begun to realize that his significant other does not share his beliefs.

Moreover, while Colin might try to offer Patricia useful ideas and suggestions for putting an end to her procrastinating ways based on what he believes is common sense, Patricia does not seem to appreciate what Colin has to offer. "Try looking at it this way," Colin said one day, in an attempt to boost Patricia's sub-basement spirits, "After you've balanced your checkbook, you can say to yourself, 'Well, I'm glad that's done and out of the way!'" However, not unsurprisingly, Patricia doesn't see things the same way due to her belief that many of her tasks are far too complex for her to deal with, let alone successfully complete. You see, deep inside, where her core beliefs lie, Patricia is so utterly convinced that she's incapable of generating a successful outcome, she's unwilling to give almost any task that requires effort an honest try. As you can imagine, this causes Colin immense frustration.

What Colin is unaware of are Patricia's self-beliefs and internal talk that support her habit of procrastinating. For example, Patricia not only believes that she's incapable of certain tasks, she's also concerned about what might happen if she were to accomplish any of her "impossible tasks." This is due to of a variety of reasons:

> ➤ Patricia believes that if she were to successfully complete a task she previously though herself incapable of completing, she might be asked to take on other unpleasant tasks.

> ➤ Patricia also believes that if she completes tasks she's avoided up until now, she'll no longer have the crucial evidence she needs to prove her assertion that she's incapable of tackling certain tasks. Ironically, Patricia doesn't seem to realize that the crucial evidence she holds onto doesn't really exist. After all, if she never tries to complete an unpleasant task, that doesn't necessarily prove that she's less capable than someone else is; all that means is that she's never really tried.

> ➤ Patricia also worries that if she ever were to accomplish one of her impossible tasks, she'd be disproving her worst critic, "herself," which to her would mean: she could have done them all along.

> ➤ Over time, Patricia has grown dependent on Colin to take care of the tasks that she'd rather not deal with. Having this luxury, Patricia may not be too interested in regaining her adulthood, her independence, or her freedom because she's become comfortable with having her needs taken care of. However, what Patricia isn't aware of is that Colin harbors resentments against her for what he believes is her refusal to pull her own weight.

Patricia's way of thinking is understandable—after all, she's put a great deal of effort into avoiding whichever tasks she finds complicated, annoying, or are boring to her in some way. This is because, deep down, Patricia doubts that she has the ability to act like a "normal" adult, like her counterpart, Colin. And, why shouldn't Patricia feel this way? After all, who among us would want to disprove something we've worked so hard, and for such a long time, to believe in as true?

In addition, Patricia perceives of her tasks as her problems, and she drags her problems around with her, day-in and day-out, refusing to deal with any of them until she's forced to acquiesce by an external entity, such as a payment due date, or an application deadline. Patricia's reliance on this kind of deadline alarm clock still isn't guaranteed to be effective. As she'd ruefully admit, there have been many times when good opportunities have slipped through her fingers, just like cans of food going past their expiration dates simply from sitting unused. Sometimes, this has less to do with procrastination, and more to do with the fact that Patricia never learned good or practical organizational skills.

How the Procrastinator's Significant Other May Feel

Colin is not amused by Patricia's behavior, and in the time that he's come to know her, he's begun wondering whether she might be using him because he sometimes feels like he's being taken advantage of. Moreover, Colin's not only noticed that Patricia handles fewer and fewer household chores, he's also picked up on the bleak outlook upon life that she seems to have acquired as of late. As a result of this observation, Colin now misses the old Patricia that he once knew, the Patricia who was joyous and seemed to beam with light.

What Can the Procrastinator and Non-Procrastinator Do To Strengthen Their Relationship?

Colin needs to talk to Patricia about his feelings of dissatisfaction and his concerns about being used. If Patricia willingly listens to Colin and takes into account that he feels that he's been unfairly burdened, that would be a great start. Then, it might be helpful if they put their heads together and made a list of some of the relatively easy household tasks that Patricia could take responsibility for. Patricia's decision to undertake her tasks could go a long way towards relieving Colin of the resentments he's felt as a result of shouldering all their household chores. In addition, when Patricia demonstrates responsibility for those tasks that she has agreed to, both she and Colin will feel that their partnership is stronger than ever.

This doesn't mean that Patricia needs to be concerned about overcoming her habitual procrastination overnight: remember, no one could make such a speedy transformation because overcoming habitual procrastination is a process that takes place over a long period of time. Patricia only needs to concern herself with whatever household tasks she's agreed to take on. However, Patricia does need to abide by the first Golden Rule of Overcoming Procrastination, which appears in Chapter Nine of this book: "Always keep the promises that you make with yourself." We can also place this Golden Rule in the context of a relationship by modifying it to say, "Always keep the promises that you make between yourself and your partner."

However, should Patricia ignore that first Golden Rule by not taking care of the tasks that she agreed to because she found other things to do with her time, Colin is quite apt to feel betrayed, and who could blame him for feeling that way? Colin needs to see proof of a change in Patricia's behavior, and should he not see that change, it's likely that he'll lose trust in her, and their relationship could suffer for it.

The Procrastinator in the Workplace

Jane is the manager of the accounting department in a mid-sized firm, and Sandy is a bookkeeping clerk in her department who happens to be a habitual procrastinator. When it comes to bookkeeping, Sandy is as skilled as any other bookkeeper in the department; however, Jane is not pleased with Sandy's overall performance.

As manager, Jane is required to write an annual evaluation for each employee in her department and to then discuss each evaluation with her superior before presenting the evaluation to each worker. Here's a shortlist of Jane's observations of Sandy:

> ➤ "Sandy avoids work. She not only wastes time and is inefficient, but she doesn't pitch in when co-workers are busy, which is something I've asked her to do on countless occasions."

> ➤ "Sandy is also a persistent latecomer. She's late almost each and every day. In fact, if I were asked what Sandy's most consistent quality was, I would have to say it was her lateness."

> ➤ Jane concludes her evaluation with this personal assessment: "I'm sorry to say the following, but we're understaffed in the accounting department and every worker there needs to perform a certain amount of work. It's my opinion that Sandy's good for excuses. Instead of getting things accomplished, she runs around in circles. Sandy seems a lot more concerned about her own welfare, than that of our organization. In short, Sandy's attitude is quite poor."

It's not terribly difficult to predict that Sandy's future with this organization may not last very long. If there's a departmental cutback, Sandy will most likely lose her role, or management could decide to take a chance on finding someone new who might show more drive than Sandy has.

Is There Anything that Sandy Can Do to Prevent Losing Her Job?

As long as Sandy has her position with this firm, there's always a chance that she might change her ways. However, in realistic terms, there's very little chance that she'll do so, because Sandy has been quite set in her ways for quite a while. It's sad to say, but there are persons who only change their ways after suffering a profound and personal setback that causes them to take stock of their situation, and of themselves.

Let's imagine that Sandy sits down in Jane's office for her annual evaluation and receives a copy of a document describing her performance, which Jane reads aloud to her. After hearing her poor evaluation, Sandy asks, "Is there anything I can do to improve?" Here's what Jane might say:

"Sandy, I'm glad to see that you're taking this evaluation seriously. We hired you to do be a bookkeeper in our department, and frankly, you haven't been doing your share of the work. But that work still needs to be done, so the only solution has been for others to do portions of your work. I want you to take note of the following suggestions, and I hope to see an improvement in your performance:

> ➢ "You need to become more of a worker amongst workers. If you see that another bookkeeper looks like he or she is buried in paperwork and you have nothing urgent on your desk, ask him or her if you can lend a helping hand. Please make an effort to pitch in."

> ➢ "My second point may come as a surprise to you, but we're very aware that you've been coming in late almost every morning. We're simply not in a position where we can allow you to come to work late every day, because if we let you do that, then we'd have to let everyone else do the same. In addition, there are people in the accounting department who have complained to me about your latenesses. They've asked if you've been given special privileges because they feel resentful that you've been getting away with coming in late, when they make a concerted effort to arrive at work on time. Please make an effort starting tomorrow to come in on time."

> ➢ "If someone criticizes your work or points out an error, try to take it as a helpful suggestion so that everyone benefits from it, and try not to make excuses for any errors on your part. We all make a mistake every now and then, that's why pencils have erasers!"

> ➢ "If you find that you're puzzled by a task that you're working on, bring it to the attention of someone who's been with the department for a longer time than you have. They'll tell you what to do, and that's a lot better than trying to figure it out on your own, and then running around in circles without an answer. There's no shame in not knowing how to do certain functions, because you're still relatively new here."

To overcome procrastination doesn't merely mean keeping busy at times when you used to goof off, it also means adopting a new way of life by not only being productive for your own sake, but for the people in your life as well. Whether the persons you interact with are close to you, or are colleagues in the workplace, being helpful to others is just as important as when you "do" tasks to help yourself.

Chapter Fifteen

Helping the Procrastinating Student

I N THE LAST CHAPTER, WE looked at close relationships between habitual procrastinators and non-procrastinators at home and in the workplace. We'll now focus our attention on helping students who procrastinate.

When it comes to the subject of habitual procrastination and the student, parents are often more concerned about their child's procrastinating ways than their child may be. This makes sense in an odd way—after all, if their child were truly concerned about his or her schoolwork, he or she probably wouldn't be procrastinating in the first place. In any event, it's always good when a parent notices any behavior in their child that has the potential to grow into a bad habit: whether it's linked to the schoolroom, or not.

Habitual procrastination can prevent a grade school student from developing a solid foundation of concentration and learning, and it can also affect a high school student's college plans, a college studeznt's career plans, or a returning student's ability to obtain a General Equivalency Diploma (G.E.D.) or new job skills.

Why Do Students Procrastinate?

Students procrastinate for many of the same reasons that adults do, however, the biggest difference between the two is found in the consequences of their in-actions. While an adult may suffer with an untidy home, it can usually be transformed into relative neatness, if only temporarily; however, a student who procrastinates may be followed by an educational transcript that reflects poorly upon him or her for some time to come. So, the old joke, "This will go down on your permanent record," might offer little to laugh about.

Here are some typical reasons for why a student may procrastinate:

➤ Because he or she never developed good study habits.
➤ The student finds a particular subject to be boring and then treats it as a low priority by avoiding it.
➤ A student finds a subject too complicated and, instead of dealing with the material, he or she backs away from it.
➤ A student may use procrastination as an improvised method for coping with stress. This approach could be called, "out of sight, is out of mind."
➤ If procrastination has gone on for a long enough, the student may not be aware of any other ways of dealing with difficult schoolwork and projects.

How Do Students Procrastinate?

Back when I was a student, there weren't nearly as many ways for someone to procrastinate as there are today. Back then, you might have the opportunity to have a long telephone call, to hang out on a street corner with friends, to watch one of the eight or nine broadcast television stations, or to stay up late listening to a transistorized AM radio tucked underneath your pillow.

Today, thanks to newer technologies and devices that have an almost instant appeal to younger folk, there are more ways to bide one's time unproductively than ever before. Some of these potential distractions are:

➤ Cell phones.
➤ Text messages.
➤ The Internet.
➤ E-mail.
➤ Chat rooms.
➤ Instant messaging.
➤ Social networking tools, like Twitter and Facebook.
➤ Portable video games.
➤ Hundreds of television channels via cable, satellite, or via the Internet.

Each of these devices has the power to dominate anyone's time, and if your child has difficulty saying "no" to any of these distractions, then it's you, the parent, who will need to take control of the situation.

Procrastination and the Grade School Student

I once spoke with a woman who said that her young daughter procrastinated with regard to her home reading assignments. She said this was because her child experienced difficulty concentrating in silence when she tried to sit down and read.

If you are reading this book specifically because you are trying to help a child who seems to have fallen into the habit of procrastination, you may have come directly to this chapter without reading the chapters that have appeared before it. If this is the case with you, then you may not have seen a point that has been repeated many times within this book, the observation that "Patience is the enemy of procrastination."

It's often the case that a people will procrastinate when they have a sense of urgency concerning a task, especially a task that they perceive as being boring, complicated, or that holds no interest for them. One of the best ways that I have found to overcome procrastination is by slowly developing patience from within. This is something that you can teach your child to do by simply sitting down with he or she and demonstrating that a task can be worked through slowly and methodically. For an interesting example of a time when I personally witnessed the positive power of patience in an academic setting, read: "Many Procrastinators Find Themselves Easily Distracted From Their Tasks" which appears as section eight, within Chapter Four.

If your child's procrastination involves difficulty in reading or studying in silence, one good way to help your child is to simply sit down with him or her, and silently read along with your child. Have your child read one line silently, and then ask him or her explain its meaning back to you. Then, continue on in that manner, line by line, reading in silence, and then stopping after each sentence, with your child relating to you what he or she believes the author is communicating to the reader.

Should you have a different view on what's been read, communicate that, and show your child that different people can view the same passages in different ways. This will also show your child that you're not asking him or her to do something that you're unwilling to do yourself. Be sure to point out to your child that he or she is able to work in silence and is capable of critically thinking about, and retaining, what they've read. You'll not only be giving your child important new skills, you'll also be increasing the amount of quality time that you spend with your child. In doing that, your child will feel important and loved, and you'll have an opportunity to get to know the person that your child is growing into.

Here are some additional suggestions for helping children who procrastinate:

> ➤ Let your child see that completing a simple task can be fun by making an enjoyable game out of it.
>
> For instance, you might suggest that you both play "The Completion Game." Give your child a task, and then ask him or her to guess the last step of the task before commencing action on it. Many people find it easier to begin working on a task when they have a mental picture of the last step involved in completing that task. Often, once the procrastinator has the first and last steps of a task in mind, the remaining steps fall into place.
>
> For more about this, read "Think 'Beginning and End,'" in Chapter Thirteen.

> ➤ Try making your child's school assignments interesting and exciting. One way to do this is to get to know your child's interests, and then try relating their school work to those things that he or she pays a lot of attention to.

> ➤ Keep track of your child's tasks and reward him or her with verbal praise for each task completed. In addition, ask your child to mentally reward him or herself every time he or she completes a task.

> ➤ Teach your child by setting an example. Demonstrate that you're not asking him or her to do anything that you're not willing to do yourself.

> ➤ Have frequent communication with your child's teacher. Know what subjects are being taught and what is being expected academically.

> ➤ If necessary, seek the assistance of your school's social worker or guidance counselor.

> ➤ Read books that deal with developing positive parenting skills.

Remember: demonstrating to your child that they can learn to develop patience within themselves doesn't just apply to reading, writing, arithmetic and other subjects in the schoolroom. Learning how to curb impatience and the frustration that often accompanies it, is vital if your child is to grow into a healthy adult who's prepared for the challenges he or she will likely face as a partner in a relationship, as an employee, and in everyday life.

Procrastination and the Teenager

It's often our friends who notice our peculiarities long before we do, and such was the case when a high school classmate said to me: "You never finish anything, Dave." Feeling that I was being unfairly criticized, I vehemently denied his allegation, but he immediately backed up his statement with proof: "For example, you start reading a book, but you never finish it; and then you start reading a new book!" Many years went by before I discovered that not only was my friend correct, but that his observation was shrewdly on-target.

High school students face an entirely different set of pressures than younger children, and many of these pressures are societal. For example, in just about every state, a high school student may drop out of school if he or she meets the age requirement. There's no telling just how many high school students drop out each year, if only because they never developed good study habits, or left because they felt they'd fallen too far behind in their schoolwork to ever catch up. This is one particularly good reason for students to avoid falling into the habit of procrastination.

By the time most high school graduates have completed their studies, a good many have been taught Sir Isaac Newton's First Law of Motion, which states: "An object in a state of uniform motion tends to remain in that state of motion until an external force is applied to it." We can adapt that law to fit procrastination by saying that: "A procrastinator who is not actively 'do'-ing, tends to remain motionless until an external or motivating force is applied to that procrastinator." This rule is as true for high school students, as it is for adults.

What Can a Parent Do To Help a Teen Who Procrastinates?

While no parents would deliberately raise their child to become a procrastinator, nevertheless, some parents don't know how to prevent their children from falling into that negative lifestyle. Just like adults who habitually procrastinate, many children also resist taking action until they have no other options, and because of that, they usually don't feel pride, joy, or even a sense of relief after they've completed a task they worked so hard at avoiding. More commonly, if they feel only one emotion, it's resentment against the institution or individual that has forced them into action.

As a result of this resentment, the teenaged procrastinator feels as if he were a marionette whose strings are being pulled and controlled by puppet-masters: his actions dictated by others. So, it's understandable if a teen, believing that he's constantly being coerced into taking action, might want to break free from what he perceives of as an adult world that seems intent on forever manipulating and controlling him.

What then can parents do to help their teenager who procrastinates when the teen may misinterpret that help as interference, or worse, as an attempt at control, which the teen may then seek to rebel against? Unfortunately for the teen and whatever he or she might otherwise wish, a parent's first priority is to protect their child, which includes correcting errant behaviors such as habitual procrastination. However, at the same time, parents need to be aware that their teenager's rebelliousness may actually be misdirected self-anger, coming as a consequence of his or her own procrastination, and it would probably do the teen a world of good to have this pointed out to him or her.

Like anyone else of any other age, teens can stop acting upon a task as a result of feeling overwhelmed. There are different reasons why the feeling of being overwhelmed seems to paralyze procrastinators to the degree that it does. Here are just a few of them:

> ➢ Sometimes a procrastinator will feel overwhelmed after convincing himself that he can't possibly accomplish a particular task because:
>   - The task is too complicated.
>   - The procrastinator believes that he lacks the sufficient intelligence, motivation, or intestinal fortitude necessary to accomplish the task.
>   - While stuck in negative and defeating self-talk, many procrastinators constantly compare themselves to fellow students who seem *better than* or *more capable* than the procrastinator believes himself to be. This practice is called "Compare and Despair," and more can be read about this in Chapter Nine, within the section entitled, "Try Not to 'Compare and Despair'."

> ➤ There are also times when a procrastinator has put off such a large number of tasks that:
>
> - He doesn't feel up to dealing with any of his tasks, because he believes they're all equal—meaning, they're all too difficult for him to accomplish. As a result of his loss of perspective, the procrastinator can't determine which task should be dealt with first. This is a very important life skill, commonly known as "prioritization."
>
> - Not wanting to deal with any of the tasks he's already put off, the procrastinator continues doing the only thing he knows how to do well; he procrastinates even more. Then, while continuing this new round of procrastination, he berates himself non-stop for not yet having taken appropriate action. Thus, his negative self-talk becomes a substitute for action.
>
> - When he's forced to deal with an unpleasant task because of a deadline or some other kind of external threat, the procrastinator surprises himself by taking appropriate action. Then, instead of congratulating himself for meeting the deadline head-on and completing the task, he now berates himself for having had the ability to deal with the task all along. Many procrastinators in this situation will say things to themselves along the lines of, "It was so simple. Why did I make such a big deal out of it? I'm so stupid!"
>
> - For more information on how procrastinators think, read Chapter Four, "The Characteristics, Behaviors, and Traits of the Human Ostrich."

One way you can help your teenager overcome procrastination is by showing him a process called "The J.O.T. Method™," which is discussed in detail in Chapters Ten and Eleven. "J.O.T." is an acronym for **"Just One Task"** and put simply, The J.O.T. Method™ helps train a procrastinator to defeat perhaps the greatest barrier to productivity—that of feeling overwhelmed.

The J.O.T. Method™ works by teaching a procrastinator to focus on **"just one task"** by breaking a task down into its simplest components, strategically accomplishing each component, and then rewarding oneself for each small victory with proof of the procrastinator's newfound abilities. You may find that in becoming familiar with The J.O.T. Method™, you'll not only be able to help your child with their issues involving procrastination, but with any of your own as well.

It's important to teach your teen to see their tasks as manageable, because with a positive outlook upon life, they'll be more likely to develop the confidence that they'll need, and hopefully, they'll have an easier time standing on their own two feet when they reach early adulthood.

However, while keeping an eye out for your teenager's own internal reasons for procrastination, it's also necessary to watch out for any external reasons for procrastination. For example:

> ➤ If technology is driving your teenager to distraction, you may wish to consider the following suggestions:
>
> - If your teenager has the latest cell phone, the one with all those flashy gadgets that make communicating almost addictive, you may want to drop by a shop that sells used cell phones and purchase him a dependable "retro-model." If you're paying your teen's monthly cell phone bill, remind him that the primary reasons for his having a cell phone is for you and him to be able to contact each other, and so he can call for help in the event of an emergency.

> ➤ Do you know what activities your teen participates in outside of school? Does he allow countless hours to roll by while watching television, playing video games, surfing the Internet, or doing almost anything but his homework or household chores? Then try these possible solutions:
>
> - Limit home computer and television time. If necessary, go to an electronics retailer and buy timers so you can prevent these devices from being turned on while you're away.
> - If your child shows little regard for his time away from school, you may need to institute some form of monitoring by having him show you his completed homework or home-based tasks.
> - Remember: if you don't show an interest in your teenager's schoolwork, how much of a chance is there that your teenager will?

> ➢ Is your teen under too much pressure to achieve? Does he complain about any of the following conditions:
>   • Fear of failure: Is he unwilling to try because he's afraid of failing?
>   • Fear of success: Is he unwilling to try because he's fearful that a positive outcome means the prospect of greater responsibility, at the expense of his freedom?
>   • Does your teenager have enough free time to act his age and have fun? If not, he may try to *borrow time* away from his schoolwork or home responsibilities.
>   • Is your teenager rebelling against demands that he must live up to academic or vocational expectations, or the need to carry on a family tradition by entering a line of work that he has no interest in pursuing?

> ➢ Does your teenager engage in so many extracurricular activities that he fails to devote adequate time to his studies?
>   • Your teenager may not necessarily be a procrastinator if he's giving his all to a school-based club or team; however, his number one priority should be to his schoolwork.

> ➢ Does your teenager exhibit any signs of the use or abuse of alcohol or recreational drugs?
>   • Do you know the signs of alcohol or drug abuse?
>   • Does your son or daughter hang out with or associate with friends who are known in the community as drinkers or drug users?

What Can A College Student Do To Avoid Falling Into Procrastination?

The difference between high school and college is akin to the difference between day and night because of the new experiences, freedoms, and responsibilities that college brings. These changes can cause some students to feel overwhelmed and, in turn, they may resort to procrastination as a negative coping measure in order to deal with the stress they feel. Later on in this chapter, we'll look at some of the more positive coping measures that one can utilize for coping with college life; but for now, let's take a detailed look at how a freshman college student's life can differ from past educational experiences.

An entering freshman needs to understand that he might not only face academic challenges, he could also encounter social challenges that may require a certain amount of adjusting to. Here are a few of those areas, accompanied by strategies and solutions:

> For students attending college away from home:
> - You'll likely reside in a dormitory, and you may find yourself sharing your room with one or more of your fellow students. Therefore, you might want to polish your diplomatic or interpersonal skills.
> - If one of your roommates likes to listen to loud music at certain times, you may want to find a dependably quiet area where you can study undeterred. Even better, see if your school will allow you to put in a request ahead of your first semester for the kind of roommate that would be a good match for you.
> - You may be allowed to prepare microwaveable dishes in the dormitory, which could help you save money; however, you wouldn't want to exist on a diet that consists solely of reheated frozen dinners. So, it might be a good idea to take a cooking course before leaving for college. Fresh food is often cheaper than prepared meals.

> In many, if not all colleges, students set their own schedules by picking which classes they'll attend and at what times. Learn how to do this ahead of time by asking someone who's familiar with the process, and keep the following suggestions in mind:
> - In order to make your first semester as trouble-free as possible, have an idea as to what courses you might like to take, and have second choices at the ready.
> - Be sure to fit study time into your overall schedule.
> - Learn how to use a class syllabus ahead of time. It will help you to stay on-track during the entire semester.

> Be aware of the following potential hazards:
> - Avoid the temptation to load up your schedule with relatively easy classes, which could make future semesters more difficult.
> - Avoid the temptation to socialize at the expense of your class work, especially on weekends.
> - Avoid the temptation to skip lectures or classes where attendance is not normally taken.

Here are some suggestions that may help college students avoid acquiring bad work habits:

> ➤ Try to get a realistic picture of college life and expected class workloads before your first semester starts by inquiring about them when you visit schools that you're considering.

> ➤ Find out who your faculty and student advisors are, and seek their counsel.

> ➤ Join study groups because you'll share study time with fellow classmates and have an opportunity to share ideas and make new acquaintances.

> ➤ Be certain to:
>   • Eat well.
>   • Get adequate rest.
>   • Exercise in order to stay fit and to defeat stress.

The Need To Make Sacrifices

While writing this book, I worked as an administrative assistant in order to pay my bills. Once, while having a conversation with a kindly lawyer that I was working with, I mentioned how many activities I'd given up in order to write this book. I then asked him whether he had ever made any sacrifices during the three years when he attended law school.

After gently laughing, he said, "There are times today when I feel like watching a movie at home. Sometimes I'll notice a film in the listings that has a good story line or some great actors in it, and I'll think to myself, 'That's funny. I don't remember *that* movie.' And then I'll look at the year the movie had been released, and I'll say to myself, 'It figures! It came out when I was in law school!'" He then went on to explain that during those three years of post-graduate education, he made a firm decision to put his social life on hold in order to concentrate on learning the law. That made me feel much better about the many sacrifices that I had already made and would continue to make in order to complete this book. For more about this concept, you may wish to read the section "Become Willing To Make Sacrifices," which appears in Chapter Thirteen.

Procrastination and the Returning Student

By definition, a "returning student" is an adult who has been away from school for a number of years. Adults return to school for a variety of good reasons—here are a few of them:

> ➤ To obtain a high school general equivalency diploma (G.E.D.)

> ➤ To acquire new skills for use in the workplace.

> ➤ To pursue a college degree while working full-time.

Because returning students are adults, many of them have responsibilities that younger students don't yet have, such as:

> ➤ The need to hold down a job to provide income.

> ➤ Paying a mortgage or rent, in addition to car payments, insurance, and household utilities.

> ➤ Taking care of children or other dependents.

Just like their younger counterparts, returning students also need to be wary of falling into procrastination, but for different reasons. Let's look at each type of returning student, and what they need to be concerned with in regard to procrastination:

> ➤ The G.E.D. student may have dropped out of high school because he or she fell so far behind in their studies, they reached a point where they decided to leave school rather than to continue battling with academic subjects.
>
> - They see that decision as having been poorly thought-out and impulsive because they are now at an economic disadvantage, and they now see obtaining their general equivalency diploma as the first step towards securing a better future for themselves. These returning students need to avoid repeating the mistakes they made in high school, and key among these choices is staying on top of their studies to avoid falling behind in their class work once more.
> - What might best help the returning G.E.D. student would be to find a specialized tutor before returning to school, for lessons on how to become a more effective student.

> ➢ Some adult students return to school for a short time in order to acquire new workplace skills by entering into "certificate programs," where the student is awarded a certificate that attests to their knowledge and/or vocational skills after passing a qualifying exam, or a series of exams.
>
>   • These courses are often taught at a fast pace, and the school may wish to maximize the number of students in each class in order to maximize their profits. So while each student is given an opportunity to learn, they may not have as much of an opportunity to ask questions as they'd like, because their instructor may be under pressure to move forward. This can foster pressure within any student who isn't prepared, which can lead to procrastination, poor performance, or even withdrawing from the course. However, there are a few things that a prospective student can do to increase their chances of success:
>
>   • Prospective students can choose their school wisely by personally visiting a few schools and interviewing their faculty, rather than simply relying upon school catalogs or brochures.
>
>   • In addition, because these programs are often taught at a quick pace, students might want to begin familiarizing themselves with the course's materials ahead of the first day of classes. One good starting point would be to see if you can purchase the books and instruction materials that will be used in the course in advance, and to then familiarize yourself with them before classes begin.

> ➢ Pursuing a college degree while working full-time is an undertaking that requires commitment and the willingness to make sacrifices over the long-term. In order to be successful, returning students could benefit from the following:
>
>   • Support from their immediate family or loved ones. This could mean asking the kids to cooperate by keeping quiet when their parent is studying.
>
>   • Having a quiet area in which to work, with a good desk, chair, and proper lighting.
>
>   • Making time to enjoy life, and to get into the sunshine every now and then.

One final subject area that we should examine concerns the relationship between procrastination and academic competition.

Some students not only want to garner their own best grades—they also want to out-"do" their fellow classmates. However, when the shoe is on the other foot, and it's the highly competitive student who has been outdone, that student may feel envy, contempt, or have a resentment against those who did better than he or she. While these negative emotions are part of the human condition, they don't necessarily help us because of their ability to distract us from our primary purpose for attending school—which is, to learn.

While there's nothing inherently wrong with wanting to do one's personal best, anyone who has had a history of battling procrastination may want to be on the lookout for signs of perfectionism within him or herself. For example: feeling the need to catch up with a classmate's grades, or having an overwhelming interest in the academic ranking of their fellow students.

One way to fend off these negative feelings of envy, contempt, and resentment is to turn the situation around by looking for the positive qualities that your fellow students have, and to then consider incorporating those attributes into your schoolwork. Always remember—your willingness to improve upon your life, is your greatest attribute.

Chapter Sixteen

Review

Ａ HABITUAL PROCRASTINATOR IS LIKE a sniper who never pulls his trigger, while forever waiting for a better shot. This is because a habitual procrastinator's initial approach to his tasks is usually to hesitate and evaluate, rather than facing and embracing those tasks he considers boring, complicated, or otherwise unappealing. This makes procrastination one of the only aspects of human behavior that is dependent upon someone *not* taking action.

Many habitual procrastinators only take action when they have no alternative but to deal with a task they've worked hard at evading, and usually expend much more mental and emotional energy in avoiding it than they would have if they'd only dealt with that task in a timely manner. As a result of this, habitual procrastinators often feel as if they're continually being hounded into taking action by creditors, spouses, bosses, governmental agencies, and other externalities. This causes procrastinators not only to have resentments against these external forces, but against their tasks as well; in turn, this can make a procrastinator feel like fleeing from just about any form of personal responsibility.

However, as the habitual procrastinator evades more tasks, he builds up a plethora of things that await his action, and the more he avoids, the less capable he tends to feel. This situation often reaches a point where the procrastinator begins to believe that he is a defective person. "After all," he thinks, "Other people seem to get their tasks accomplished, other people have homes that are clean and organized; and, other people get things done." If a procrastinator thinks along those lines for long enough, he will not only lose confidence in his abilities, he can also lose his self-esteem and fall victim to mental depression. In addition, with the unrelenting pressure that comes from an ever-mounting burden of undone tasks, many habitual procrastinators also face difficulties with feelings of anxiety.

Paradoxically, there are some procrastinators who perform well in the workplace, but stare in bewilderment at what they see as unmanageable messes at home. Instead of taking action upon their sea of domestic untidiness, they feel sad at the thought of "losing an entire weekend to housecleaning" when taking that action might otherwise lift their spirits. Still, many procrastinators who have reached this point have already lost the ability to do routine housekeeping, often to such a degree that they would no longer associate the word "routine" with the word "housekeeping." In short, a habitual procrastinator not only loses confidence in his decision-making ability, but also feels overwhelmed by life.

Knowing only the pressure of the tasks that lay ahead of him, the procrastinator may resort to "floating," or the taking of lengthy rest breaks, which are actually "mini-crashes" or flights from life's responsibilities by engaging in distractions like aimless television viewing, surfing the Internet, daydreaming, and oversleeping.

Procrastinators need to learn how to calm themselves down by engaging in sensible self-talk, and by breaking their tasks down into manageable components, such as by using The J.O.T. Method™, which provides procrastinators with a list of the tasks they've completed, and those that they haven't yet accomplished. Having a workable mechanism like The J.O.T. Method™ not only helps us accomplish our tasks, but it also provides us with reassurance that the work we've done "counts," and that the tasks we weren't able to get to will not disappear, because they exist on paper to be completed another day. By using The J.O.T. Method™, we train ourselves to think incrementally by writing our tasks down so we can see what we've done, and what we haven't gotten around to yet.

Writing our tasks down also provides us with something that we never had in the past, and which is crucially important to fighting procrastination: positive feedback. When we were procrastinating, our minds were constantly fixed upon the tasks that awaited our attention, and which we were avoiding; so, even when we accomplished a task, we never saw that as progress. We couldn't bask in the joy that can come from a job well done because our attention was consumed by our desire to escape all the rest of our undone tasks.

As practicing procrastinators, we often experienced mixed feelings after successfully accomplishing a task, because after having convinced ourselves that we were incapable of dealing with it, to then accomplish it by taking appropriate action might mean that we had the ability all along. We then feel dismayed at ourselves, because essentially, we've burst our own bubble. This conflict not only generates negative feelings within ourselves, but those negative feelings can also be directed outside ourselves as well; they most commonly take the form of resentments against the person or institution that forced us to take action. Indeed, even if that action were in our own best interest, it often only strengthens our resolve to fight against the forces that seem bent upon keeping us down.

However, if we put our tasks, our thoughts, our situations, and our dilemmas down on paper, we can examine and re-examine them, along with the actions that we took, which will show us how we went about solving the problems that once confounded us. Then, instead of feeling as if we've somehow betrayed our conscious resolve by taking action, positive feedback replaces our old negative self-talk, which allows us to take delight in our newfound abilities.

If we allow ourselves to enjoy the positive process of changing from habitual procrastination, and into more active lives, our outlook upon our tasks may change as well. Here's a list of some of the different types of positive changes that you may experience as you start to recover from procrastination:

➤ **Personal Satisfaction:** Our reasons for taking action change. Instead of acting as a last resort in order to avoid a negative consequence, such as paying your electric bill to prevent your electricity from being shut off, you promptly pay your bills in order to maintain the great feeling that comes from staying on top of things.

➤ **Less Frustration:** In the past, we easily became frustrated at tasks that were not easily dealt with. In time, we came to understand that even the tasks we initially predicted would pose no problems, often took more time than we had estimated. Now, instead of allowing ourselves to become flustered, we work at developing our own level of patience, we learn to make allowances for things that don't happen to go our way, and we allocate extra time to new projects, in case that they take more time than we anticipated. In short, we find that the more we increase our level of patience, the more that we feel capable of handling.

➤ **Finally, We Feel Like Dealing With It:** Rather than waiting for the right time to come along, when we'll feel like dealing with a task, we realize that we don't usually feel like dealing with something until after we've begun dealing with it. It can take time to internalize this concept, but after you get it, it becomes undeniably clear—that no matter how unappealing a task may seem, once you begin working on that task, it's then, and only then, when you feel like getting it finished and out of the way.

➤ **We Feel Secure and Confident:** Instead of clinging to procrastination as a security blanket that helps us avoid the things we're afraid of dealing with, we see procrastination is an "insecurity blanket" which causes us to feel less emotionally secure, and makes us doubt our capabilities. In time, instead of purposely avoiding our tasks, we frown upon this negative reaction and look forward to seeing how well we can deal with something that formerly brought us to a complete stop or severely challenged us.

➤ **We Now Have a Roadmap:** Distractions no longer have the immense powers that they once had to keep us from our tasks. This is because our tasks no longer pose the threat to our peace of mind and self esteem that they once did. Instead, we now know how to effectively deal with our tasks, because as we gain experience in dealing with them and crossing them off of our J.O.T. lists, we see our results and feel stronger than we used to. In addition, if something unexpectedly comes up, our J.O.T. list serves as a roadmap that we can always refer back to. This is very different from how we behaved in the past, when we tried to come back from a distraction and hadn't a clue on how to proceed.

> **Contentment:** We start seeing "do"-ing as an opportunity to experience feelings of contentment. We look forward to setting a period of time aside to deal with our tasks because we like the changes that come from accomplishing things. We see these changes in the neatness of our living spaces, which are now clean and organized. We find things with far less effort, and on those occasions when we see that we're perhaps not as organized as we wish we were, we do something about it by thinking up a solution, and taking action. For example, this could mean creating a file folder so you know where important papers are, buying a bookshelf unit in order to have the space to decorate your home in a way that pleases you, or finding other solutions that make your living space work for you.

> **Capability:** We discover that we're far more capable than we had ever imagined ourselves to be. Being capable in this way does not necessarily mean that we go around cleaning in a manic or frantic way, but that we react to our tasks with less hesitation by welcoming the completion of the task within our own minds. We allow ourselves time off to relax, and enjoy the sense of control that we finally have over our personal time.

Looking back on how far we've come, we see many differences between how we used to live and the lives we now lead. As procrastinators, we rewarded ourselves for not dealing with our tasks by fixating our attention on false options. Today, we look at work as its own reward, with each task as an opportunity to better our lives.

In the past, I lived an irresponsible life and felt terrible for it. Today, I'm surprised that my typical response to feeling overwhelmed by depression and anxiety back then was to ask myself, "Why me?" or "Why is this happening to me?" I've changed from a person who was constantly trying to evade both my responsibilities and the consequences of my in-actions, into someone who generally doesn't need to concern himself with the consequences of not having taken care of a task, because he's already dealt with it.

Earlier, in Chapter Four, we discussed "The 25 Aspects of Procrastination," where the traits of habitual procrastinators were detailed. Here now is a more positive list of suggestions to take with you as you finish this book and move forward into your life as a non-procrastinator:

25 Suggestions to Help Make Your Life Procrastination-Free

1. Always keep the promises that you make with yourself.

2. Patience is the enemy of procrastination. Work at developing patience within yourself.

3. Plan your work—and work your plan.

4. Gambling with our responsibilities is always a false-option.

5. Avoid the temptation of diversions that are false options and time wasters.

6. When dealing with tasks, avoid creating new work for yourself by always doing a complete action.

7. There are times when any action is better than in-action. Should procrastination ever immobilize you, the best course of action to take, is to take action.

8. Remember: What gets measured, gets done.

9. You're always guaranteed to be right when you have an excuse.

10. Perfect doesn't exist. For a recovering procrastinator, *good enough is great!*

11. Yard-by-yard is hard, but inch-by-inch, and it's a cinch!

12. Feelings aren't facts. While feelings can be terribly uncomfortable and may seem real, they only represent our interpretation of how we perceive our situation.

13. Housecleaning is a mood changer.

14. Disorganized thinking creates disorganized actions.

15. Incorporate exercise into your life, because nothing can get you moving—like movement.

16. Over-analysis leads to paralysis.

17. By making something a priority, it becomes a priority.

18. Forward movement fights depression.

19. Don't analyze –utilize.

20. Be gentle with yourself.

21. If a task has you down because it's particularly complicated, boring, or frustrating, work at converting it into an exciting challenge by using one of the advanced techniques described earlier in Chapter Thirteen.
22. Work at developing patience from within by repeating the word "patience" to yourself, like it were a mantra. Or, develop your own mantra.
23. If you must stop working on a task before it's been completed, then place the remaining parts of that task on tomorrow's J.O.T. List: that way, you'll already have a plan for what to "do" tomorrow.
24. Today's sacrifice equals tomorrow's success.
25. You can't think your way into good action, but you can act your way into good thinking.

In closing, this isn't the end, because for you, it's only the beginning—the start of a whole new you! Because of this, I'd like to end with a few thoughts that made their first appearance in the closing of this book's Introduction:

All that changing from a procrastinator, and into a "do"-er takes, is the willingness on your part to challenge your beliefs. As you gradually incorporate changes into your life, new feelings of self-esteem and personal pride will replace old feelings of depression and gloom which came about as a result of not taking care of your needs. Even if you've grown concerned that you may have lost the ability to act on your own behalf, I can assure you that you can regain a great deal more control over your life than you might otherwise believe. This has been my own experience.

It is my sincere and heartfelt hope that this book helps you to start undertaking the tasks you've been putting off. In the end, not only will you become a "do"-er, you'll also discover that taking care of yourself generates good feelings that you'll come to relish.

So then, "How many procrastinators does it take to change a light bulb?" The answer is: "None. Procrastinators sit in the dark!"

I wish you every success on your journey into the light!

Index

Notes

Notes

Notes

Notes

Breinigsville, PA USA
29 August 2010
244455BV00005B/3/P